THE DANGEROUS
BOOK OF
DINOSAURS

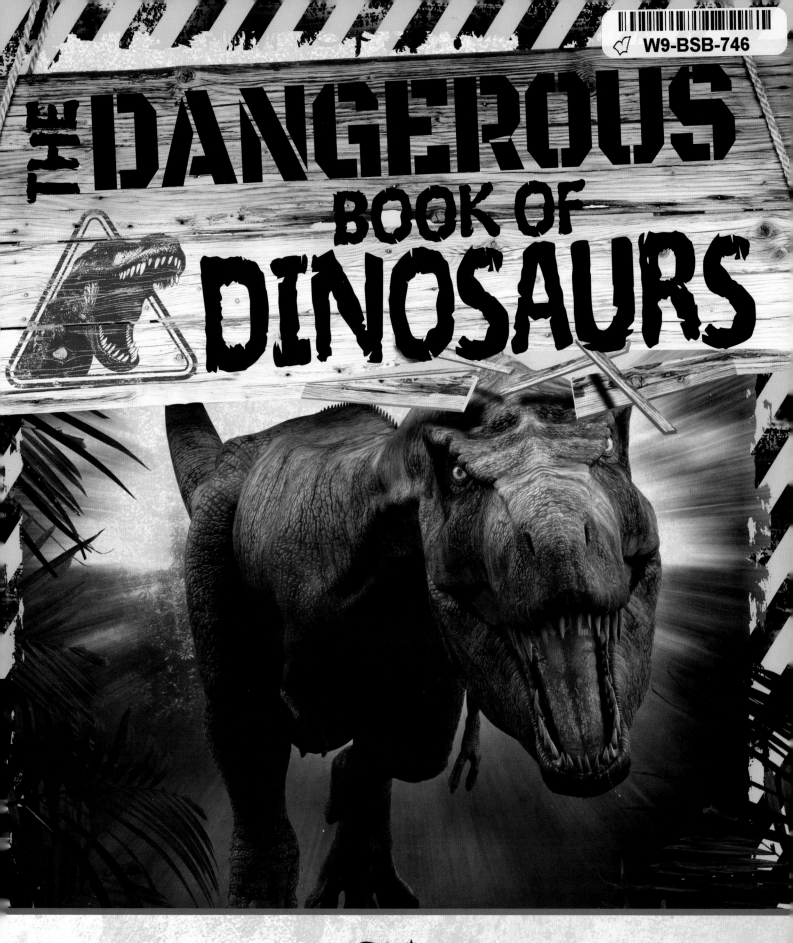

ARCTURUS

ARCTURUS

This edition published in 2015 by Arcturus Publishing Limited
26/27 Bickels Yard, 151–153 Bermondsey Street,
London SE1 3HA

ISBN: 978-1-78404-196-0
CH004188NT
Supplier: 26, Date 1015, Print run 4621

Author: Liz Miles
Editors: Joe Harris, Alex Woolf and Joe Fullman
Designer: Emma Randall
Original design concept and cover design: Notion Design

Picture Credits:
Key: b-bottom, m-middle, l-left, r-right, t-top
All images by pixel-shack.com except for:
Shutterstock: p6, br, bl; p7 br; p8 bl; p9 mr; p11 br; p13 bl; p15 t; p19 tr;
p21 br; p25 tr; p25 m; p28 br; p35 tr; p53 br; p55 cr; p65 b; p71 br; p89;
br; p91 mr; p105 br; p109 br; p111 br; p112 br; p123 br.
Wikipedia Commons: p45 br; p51 br; p59 br; p79 tl; p96 ml; p103 t.

Printed in China

CONTENTS

DINOSAUR PLANET

The dinosaurs were a group of reptiles that ruled the Earth for over 160 million years. They ranged from giant hunters, such as Spinosaurus (SPINE-oh-SORE-us) to tiny speedsters, like Compsognathus (comp-sog-NATH-us).

Plant-eating dinosaurs were in constant danger from savage meat-eaters. Some dinosaurs, like hadrosaurs (HAD-roh-sores), roamed in herds. Others, like Euoplocephalus (YOU-oh-plo-SEFF-ah-luss) were most likely solitary.

Dinosaurs lived at different times. Some of the best known dinosaurs, such as the fearsome hunter Tyrannosaurus rex (tie-RAN-oh-SORE-us REX), and the horned Triceratops (try-SEH-rah-tops), stalked the Earth during the Cretaceous period.

An asteroid streaks through the sky toward Earth where it will wipe out the dinosaurs (p.20).

OTHER PREHISTORIC MONSTERS

The dinosaurs may have ruled the land, but they were not the only creatures to call the prehistoric Earth their home. They lived alongside insects, mammals, and other reptiles.

During the dinosaur era, terrifying pterosaurs (flying lizards) ruled the skies, while the oceans were filled with fantastical sea monsters – aggressive reptiles, monstrous squid, and giant sharks.

Then, mysteriously, about 65 million years ago, all the dinosaurs, together with many other creatures, suddenly died out.

CHANGING EARTH

THE STORY OF OUR DYNAMIC PLANET

RED-HOT PLANET

Four and a half billion years ago, Earth had no land, oceans, atmosphere, or life. Pounded by meteorites, it became hotter and hotter until most of it was molten. But slowly, gas from inside leaked out, and an atmosphere formed. About 3.8 billion years ago, oceans began to appear.

DAWN OF LIFE

About 3.5 billion years ago, most of Earth's surface was a vast, shallow ocean. It was here that the first simple, single-celled life forms emerged. More complex, multi-celled life wouldn't evolve for another 2 billion years.

Earth today is very different from the place where dinosaurs once roamed. Our world may seem unchanging, but it is in fact in a constant state of gradual change. The planet's surface is made up of huge plates that float on a mass of molten (liquid) rock. Over millions of years, the plates slowly move, causing continents to shift, mountains to rise, and oceans to grow and shrink. Fossils show us that the land masses were arranged very differently in prehistoric times.

AGE OF THE DINOSAURS

Land masses slowly emerged. When the dinosaurs first appeared about 225 million years ago (in the Triassic period) all the continents were one giant land mass, or "supercontinent". By the time the dinosaurs died out (at the end of the Cretaceous period, 65 million years ago), the land had split up into continents that look familiar to us today.

THE MODERN WORLD

Today's Earth is still changing. The continents are still moving, species are becoming extinct, and new species are evolving.

TIMELINE

OF LIFE ON EARTH

Scientists have divided the billions of years of prehistoric time into periods. Dinosaurs lived in the Triassic, Cretaceous, and Jurassic periods, while modern humans evolved in the Quaternary period.

← CAMBRIAN
541–485 mya:
Life forms become
more complex.

↓ SILURIAN
443–419 mya:
First creatures on land.

↑ ORDOVICIAN
485–443 mya:
Arthropods (creatures with exoskeletons) rule the seas. Plants colonize the land.

↑ PRECAMBRIAN
4,570–541 million years ago (mya): The first life forms appear. They are tiny, one-celled creatures.

↑ DEVONIAN
419–359 mya: First insects, fish now dominate the seas.

↓ CRETACEOUS
145–65 mya: Spinosaurus and T. rex evolve. Dinosaur extinction.

↘QUATERNARY
2.6 mya– today: Woolly mammoths roam the Earth, modern humans evolve.

← PALEOGENE/ NEOGENE
65–2.6 mya: Many giant mammal species emerge

↓ TRIASSIC
252–201 mya: First dinosaurs.

↑ JURASSIC
201–145 mya: The largest plant-eating dinosaurs evolve.

↑ TODAY

← PERMIAN
299–252 mya: First therapsids (ancestors of mammals) evolve.

← CARBONIFEROUS
359–299 mya: Reptiles first appear, vast forests cover the land.

UNDERWATER CREATURES

The ancient seas teemed with life millions of years before the dinosaurs stalked the land. The first creatures to live in the oceans were single-celled life forms. They were followed by strange, multi-celled organisms. These gradually evolved into scary-looking marine creatures that crept, burrowed, and hunted for food.

TOP PREDATOR

Anomalocaris (a-nom-ah-lo-CA-ris), which means "abnormal shrimp", was a large and dangerous predator. It searched for prey with its two compound eyes (each with thousands of lenses) on stalks. Up to 2 m (6 ft) long, it would have been a terrifying sight. The mouth was made of crushing plates that surrounded cutting prongs. Spiked arms around the mouth would have captured its prey, and pulled it down into its barbed throat.

FIVE-EYED MONSTER

The palm-sized Opabinia (oh-pa-BIN-ee-ah) had five eyes and lived in Cambrian seas. It may also have spent a lot of time burrowing into the mud on the seabed to hunt for worms. Its long proboscis (an organ extending from its face) had grasping spines.

MYSTERIOUS SEAS

Between 635 and 545 million years ago, animal life developed from single-celled forms to soft-bodied, multi-celled forms. We don't know much about the first sea creatures. As they had no hard shells or skeletons, only a few fossils survive. Many may have looked like soft blobs, or similar to today's marine worms, jellyfish, and sea pens.

TIME DETECTIVES

Marine fossils usually come from creatures that had shells, skeletons, or exoskeletons. Ancient seabeds are sometimes uncovered when rivers cut through old rock (as in the Grand Canyon, USA). Scientists can work out the age of fossils by the layer of rock they are found in — the deeper they are buried, the more ancient they are.

EMERGING ONTO THE LAND

Fish slowly ventured onto the land, evolving the body features of amphibians, such as lungs to breathe and four legs to help them move. No one knows why some went ashore – perhaps it was to escape from hungry arthropods, or maybe they got stuck in pools that were drying out.

The first fish-like land creatures may have flopped ashore in the Devonian period. They would have dragged themselves about on adapted fins, like today's mudskippers. True, four-legged amphibians like Eyrops (EH-ree-ops) developed later.

OPEN WIDE!

About 290 million years ago, Eryops lurked in the waters – a huge, sturdy amphibian and one of the top predators of Permian times. It had no chewing teeth but did have wide-opening jaws. It must have grasped its prey and perhaps chucked it in the air until it was dead, using special teeth in the roof of its mouth. It would then have swallowed the creature whole, like a crocodile.

MUD FLOPPER

Ichthyostega (IK-thee-oh-STAY-gah) lived before Eryops, in late Devonian times. It was a weird mix of fish and amphibian. It had a fin at the end of its tail, but also had leg and toe bones. The hind legs were used like paddles, and the front limbs were probably strong enough to allow it to drag itself onto the shore and flop about on the mud like a modern-day mudskipper. It had lungs that would have allowed it to breathe air for short stretches of time.

 # TIME DETECTIVES

As fish fin prints and four-legged amphibian footprints look very different, fossil footprints are an important clue to help us find out when creatures first emerged from the water. Fossilized footprints with toes from 395 million years ago were found in Poland and are thought to be the oldest evidence of amphibians walking on the land.

EARLY REPTILES

FIERCE FORERUNNERS

Over time, the climate became drier. The vast, swampy forests of the Carboniferous period disappeared. The amphibians suffered because they needed to lay their eggs in water. Some, however, evolved into reptiles, which thrived because they could lay their eggs on land.

Early reptiles included fish-eaters with deadly teeth, like Ophiacodon (oh-fee-ACK-oh-don). Some, like Dimetrodon (die-MET-roe-don), which emerged later, had spectacular sails growing from their backs.

SNAKE TOOTH

Ophiacodon, which means "snake tooth", was one of the earliest land-based reptiles. It lived in late Carboniferous and early Permian times, and probably spent a lot of time in water, grabbing fish with its mass of tiny, sharp teeth. It probably hunted down amphibians on shore, too, including its smaller, plant-eating cousin, Edaphosaurus (eh-DAFF-oh-SORE-us). Around 3.4 m (11 ft) long, Ophiacodon was a top hunter with a powerful bite, and its only challengers were other Ophiacodons.

FIN BACK

Dimetrodon was a fierce carnivore that hunted the land for its prey 50 million years before the dinosaurs appeared. It was the biggest and probably the most aggressive creature of its time. No one knows exactly what the sail on its back was for. It might have been used to threaten competitors, and to store heat from the sun for when it was cold. On hot days it might have been used like a car radiator, to cool the creature down.

DIMETRODON

VITAL STATISTICS

Meaning of name: Two shapes of teeth

Family: Sphenacodontidae

Period: Early Permian

Size:
1.7-4.6 m / 5.6-15.1 ft length

Weight: up to 250 kg / 550 lb

Distinguishing feature:
Large, thin sail on back

Diet: Meat and insects

SAIL AWAY
Skin covered spines grew from Dimetrodon's backbone to form a sail.

QUICK MOVER
Its legs, which spread out from either side of its body, allowed it to move fast. The amphibians and reptiles it preyed on probably found it hard to escape.

FLESH-EATER
It had two types of teeth – sharp and serrated. The serrated teeth were like meat knives, ideal for tearing the flesh from its catch.

THE FIRST DINOSAURS

HUNGRY HUNTERS

Dinosaurs evolved from reptiles, and first appeared in Triassic times. The earliest dinosaurs already had many of the deadly features of the later, more famous meat-eaters. They had curved finger claws, sharp teeth, and jaws built to hold onto prey struggling to escape.

FIRST FOSSIL FINDS

Fossils of the earliest dinosaurs, such as Eoraptor (EE-owe-RAP-tore), have been found in Argentina. But they were not all top predators – the meat-eating Herrerasaurus (herr-RARE-oh-SORE-us), for example, may have itself been the prey of a bigger monster.

DAWN RAIDER

Although an early dinosaur, the fox-sized Eoraptor looked very much like the hunting dinosaurs of Jurassic times, millions of years later. It walked upright on two legs and had meat-eating jaws. Its teeth were razor sharp, small, and backward-curving, so could give a nasty bite. Its name means "dawn plunderer".

LONG IN THE TOOTH

Herrerasaurus was 5 m (16.5 ft) tall, with teeth more than twice as long as a human's and grooved like a saw for cutting. It was also equipped with sharp claws at the end of its three-fingered hands. A good sense of hearing may have helped it to find its prey, and also to listen out for an aggressor that shared the same territories: a giant crocodile-like carnivore called Saurosuchus (sore-oh-SOO-kuss).

EARLY PLANT-CHOMPER

One of the first plant-eating dinosaurs was Thecodontosaurus (thee-co-DON-toe-SORE-us), which had small, plant-cutting teeth and walked on all fours. It was as tall as an adult human and chomped away at low-growing plants.

AGE OF THE DINOSAURS

Dinosaurs ruled the world for 150 million years. The Age of the Dinosaurs covered the Triassic, Jurassic, and Cretaceous periods, together called the Mesozoic era.

The dinosaurs ranged from giant-sized to chicken-sized, and from aggressive meat-eaters to gentle, grazing plant-eaters. No land was safe from the dinosaurs – their fossils have been found on every continent, and they lived in many varied habitats, from wetlands to arid open plains, and from coastlines and lagoons to forests and deserts.

CAVERN-JAWED KILLERS

The theropods (THAIR-oh-pods) were vicious, two-legged carnivores. They included Giganotosaurus (JIG-an-OH-toe-SORE-us) and T. rex, shown here. Their jaws were huge, even compared with the head of a large sauropod like Amargasaurus (ah-MAR-gah-SORE-us). Giganotosaurus probably hunted in packs, and together would have been capable of bringing down the mighty Amargasaurus, despite the herbivore's defensive whipping tail and spiny back.

DINOSAUR DETECTIVES

A complete or near-complete fossil of a dinosaur skeleton is a rare but important find, so it has to be excavated with care. The position of each fossil bone is recorded before it is removed. Scientists then get to work reconstructing the dinosaur. Missing pieces are filled in with plaster.

LAND GIANTS

The sauropods – the heaviest, tallest, and longest animals ever to pound the Earth – lived on plants. Their tree trunk-like legs and long, stretching necks allowed them to reach high-growing plants, and their colossal size and whip-like tails intimidated the killers that stalked them. The sauropods included Apatosaurus (a-PAT-oh-SORE-us), which was four times taller than a modern giraffe.

PROTECTED BY PLATES

Plant-eaters developed ways of protecting themselves from meat-eaters. Ankylosaurus (ANK-ill-oh-SORE-us), for example, was covered in thick, bony plates, as well as spikes and studs, to shield it from the bites of hungry carnivores. It also had a clubbed tail to thwack at hunters.

EXTINCTION EVENT

Sixty-five million years ago, the dinosaurs disappeared. Many other species also died out around this time, suggesting that a sudden catastrophe made it impossible for lots of animals to survive. This could have been an asteroid or comet, volcanic eruptions, or a combination of both.

DUST CLOUDS

If a meteor hit Earth, the dust clouds would have been so thick they would have have blocked out the sun for months. Temperatures would have dropped, causing the widespread death of forests and animals.

DEEP IMPACT!

Some scientists believe that the dinosaurs died out after a giant comet or asteroid fell to Earth. It would have smashed into the Earth's crust, hurling tons of dust into the atmosphere.

VIOLENT VOLCANOES

Around the time the dinosaurs died out, there was a lot of volcanic activity in northern India. These volcanoes were emitting lava for thousands of years – the lava flows are estimated to have covered an area about half the size of India! The chemicals released from the eruptions would have had a worldwide impact, causing major changes in the Earth's atmosphere. Many scientists believe that volcanic eruptions were killing off the dinosaurs long before a comet or asteroid fell to Earth.

DINOSAUR DETECTIVES

The Chicxulub crater in Mexico, shown here in an artist's impression, provides evidence that a huge meteor impact took place. This massive crater is 180 km (112 miles) in width – the meteor that created it is thought to have been 10 km (6 miles) wide!

AFTER THE DINOSAURS

MASSIVE MAMMALS

After the dinosaurs, mammals grew to become the largest animals both on land and in the sea. They included the fearsome, curved-toothed Smilodon (SMILE-oh-don), which belonged to a family of now extinct cat-like creatures called machairodonts (mah-CARE-oh-donts).

Many mammals from the Paleogene, Neogene, and Quaternary periods looked like species that are alive today, but terrifyingly enlarged. Some, such as Smilodon, lived up to the time when humans had evolved and may have even hunted humans for food.

DEADLY SMILE

Smilodon had a deadly bite – it could open its mouth twice as wide as a modern-day lion. As well as its biting teeth, including the two huge, curved canine teeth, it had chewing teeth at the back of its jaws. This hunter may have leapt from trees or the undergrowth to ambush its prey. It would then use its powerful body to wrestle its victim to the ground and hold it there with its huge front paws, ready for one precise and deadly bite.

LOOK OUT FOR THE TAIL

Doedicurus (DAY-dih-CORE-us) was an incredible mammal from the Quaternary period that must have looked a little like a giant (and terrifying) armadillo. Its protective shell was covered in skin and may have been hairy. Males swiped their tails armed with knobs or spikes at each other in power battles. Dents from the tails have been found on the shells of some males.

DOEDICURUS
VERSUS
ARMADILLO

	DOEDICURUS	ARMADILLO
HEIGHT	1.5 m (5 ft)	0.3 m (1 ft)
LENGTH	4 m (13 ft)	1.5 m (5 ft)
WEIGHT	Up to 2,370 kg (2.6 tons)	Up to 32 kg (71 lb)
TEETH	Grinding teeth at the back	80–100 peg-shaped teeth
FOOD	Plants	Insects, small animals, plants, fruit, carrion

DESCENDANTS OF THE DINOSAURS

The closest things to dinosaurs living on our planet today are birds. Birds descended from two-legged, meat-eating dinosaurs called theropods. Scientists found the evidence for this when they made an incredible discovery – fossilized dinosaurs that had feathers.

Species like Caudipteryx (caw-DIP-ter-ix), which possessed both dinosaur and bird features, show the gradual transition from one type of animal to the other. At first, feathers were just for warmth and display, but then, through evolution, they began to be used for flight, too. Perhaps the first true bird was Archaeopteryx (are-kee-OP-ter-ix), whose fossil was discovered in 1862. Even though Archaeopteryx was more bird than dinosaur, it could probably only flutter rather than fly.

SHOWTIME TAIL

Like birds today, Caudipteryx may have spread its tail feathers to attract mates or scare off predators.

DOWNY COAT

Its feather coating was for warmth, not flight. The downy covering was discovered in fossils. It might have been marked with tones and pigments, although we can't know for sure as these rarely survive in fossils.

BIRD-LEGS

Like a modern bird, the early Cretaceous Caudipteryx may have perched on branches or used its long legs to wade into lakes or rivers.

FLIGHTLESS

The feathers on the arms were too short and the wrong shape for flight. They may have been used to keep their young warm in their nests.

DINOSAURS DOWN THE GARDEN

Of course there aren't really dinosaurs living in anyone's garden, yet there are incredible similarities between some birds today and the predatory little theropods of the Cretaceous period. Feathers, lightweight skulls, wishbones in their skeletons, and two legs for walking are some of the shared features.

MAIDEN FLIGHT

With sharp teeth and a bony tail, Archaeopteryx was similar to a theropod. Yet it also had feathers and wings that allowed it to fly, although not as well as most birds today. To fly, it probably launched itself from trees or rocks.

Seen here hunting by a waterhole, the terrifying T. rex (pp.28–29) was one of the top predators of its day.

KILLER DINOSAURS

Killer dinosaurs – the carnivores – were among the deadliest animals ever to roam this planet. They took many forms, ranging from the giant theropods with their bone-crushing jaws and flesh-ripping teeth, to the small but fleet-footed raptors with their grasping hands and slashing claws.

Carnivores used many different methods to catch and kill their prey. Some hunted alone, while others worked in packs. Some had powerful toothless beaks, while others had needle-sharp teeth. Some used speed, while others relied on enormous muscle power, deadly kicks, or super-sized bites.

SMART AND DEADLY

Meat-eating dinosaurs, such as Allosaurus (al-loh-SORE-us), shown in the picture on the left, had good eyesight, a keen sense of smell, and a large brain to plan hunting strategies. They also had long, strong legs to run fast and catch their prey. Perhaps the biggest carnivore of all was Spinosaurus (SPINE-oh-SORE-us), at about 18 m (59 ft) long. The smallest was probably Hesperonychus (HES-pare-RON-i-kus) at just 1 m (3.3 ft).

TYRANT LIZARD

Tyrannosaurus rex (tie-RAN-o-SORE-us REX) means "tyrant lizard". This terrifying creature was one of the strongest and biggest of the dinosaur predators, stalking the land in the last part of the Cretaceous period. It grew to 12 m (39 ft) in length and its jaws alone were 1.4 m (4.5 ft) long and filled with ferocious teeth the size of large daggers.

Because of its oddly weak little arms, some scientists think that T. rex fed on carrion rather than living prey. But others say that it would have needed more than carcasses to satisfy its hunger and that its forward-facing eyes were designed to spot and judge the distance of fast-moving prey.

POWER MUSCLES

Bulky muscles gave this monster incredible power and legs strong enough to carry its massive body weight of 4,500 kg (5 tons). Like an elephant, it could probably walk fast, but its weight would have made running difficult.

DINOSAUR DETECTIVES

Fossils of Tyrannosaurus rex jaws show how it had a very wide bite. There was an extra jaw joint, so that, like a snake, T. rex could almost dislocate its jaws. This would have allowed its mouth to open extraordinarily wide. The strength and thickness of the skull bones suggest it had powerful jaw muscles, strong enough to crush bones.

RAZOR TEETH
The pointed front teeth were designed for grabbing and puncturing thick skin, while the back teeth were blade shaped for sawing through bones, flesh, and muscle.

LETHAL BITE
A T. rex bite mark on the fossil of a duckbill was used to work out the power of its bite. Scientists estimate a bite force of 1,365 kg (1.5 tons), more than three times that of an African lion. Rather than battle with its prey, the T. rex's aim would have been to cripple it with one chomp. Once its prey had fallen, the bone-crushing jaws could then finish it off.

LITTLE ARMS
Although a hunter, Tyrannosaurus rex had small, weak arms, and two-fingered hands that would not have even reached its mouth! Perhaps these arms were used to steady its vast body as it stood up.

RAVENOUS GIANTS

Giganotosaurus (jig-an-OH-toe-SORE-us) was definitely gigantic – this beast was as heavy as a truck and, at 13 m (46 ft), it was longer than a T. rex. This killer dinosaur lived with the giant plant-eating titanosaurs on the South American plains, which it probably hunted.

MIND-BLOWING DISCOVERY

For a hundred years Tyrannosaurus rex was the biggest predator known, but in 1993 an even bigger one was discovered. Named Giganotosaurus, it has the longest theropod jaws ever found, measuring 1.8 m (5.9 ft) – longer than many adult humans are tall! It lived around 30 million years before T. rex and had three fingers on each hand – better for gripping than T. rex's two. Its bite was less powerful, but its blade-like cutting teeth could easily slice through skin and bone.

KILLER PAIRS

Giganotosaurus wasn't afraid to hunt creatures much bigger than itself and was probably the only predator of Argentinosaurus (AR-gen-tee-no-SORE-us), which was three times taller. Scientists believe that Giganotosaurus may have hunted in pairs or groups of six or more, using its powerful jaws to bite at the legs of the slow-moving sauropods until they weakened from bleeding and fell down. The Giganotosaurus pack would then move in to tear at the meat and consume the carcass.

GIGANOTOSAURUS

VITAL STATISTICS

Meaning of name:
Giant southern lizard

Family: Allosauridae

Period: Late Cretaceous

Size: 7 m / 23 ft height;
13 m / 46 ft length

Weight: 7,300 kg / 8 tons

Diet: Meat

HUGE HUNGER

One sauropod kill could probably have satisfied a Giganotosaurus's hunger for a few weeks. There would have been no competition from other meat-eating hunters because of Giganotosaurus's size and power. The giant predators may have been surprisingly fast, too. Scientists estimate they could have attained speeds of up to 50 km/h (31 mph).

UTAHRAPTOR

VICIOUS PACK HUNTERS

Utahraptor (YOO-ta-RAP-tor) was an intelligent, agile, and swift hunter. It had a stiff tail to help it stay balanced as it pounced on its prey. As heavy as a large bear, it was the biggest of the dromaeosaurids or "running lizards" (also called raptors).

QUITE A BITE

The Utahraptor's powerful jaws were crammed with razor-sharp teeth, which it used to bite and grasp its prey once it had pulled it down with its claws.

WHO YOU CALLIN' CHICKEN?

Fossils show a bone structure similar to a chicken's, and scientists believe it was also covered in feathers. In spite of the feathers it couldn't fly, and any feathery covering would have been for warmth, or for show to attract a mate.

KILLER CLAWS

Utahraptor's sickle-shaped claws were its prize weapons. It raised these off the ground as it ran. The 35 cm (14 in) long blades could tear at its prey or cling on like climbing crampons. With a powerful kick, the claw could have brought down another dinosaur, often killing it instantly.

Like wolves, Utahraptors stalked their prey in packs. Working together, they could have brought down even large sauropods. They would cling to their prey's bodies, biting and tearing until their victims were exhausted.

UTAHRAPTOR VERSUS WOLF

How do these pack hunters measure up?

	UTAHRAPTOR	**WOLF**
HEIGHT	3 m / 9.9 ft	0.85 m / 2.83 ft
WEIGHT	1,000 kg / 1.1 tons	60 kg / 130 lb
SPEED	30 kph / 20 mph	55-70 kph / 34-43 mph
BITE FORCE	460 kg / 1014 lbs	66 kg / 145 lbs
EYESIGHT	Excellent	Very good

SICKLE-CLAWED RUNNERS

Utahraptor belonged to a family of dinosaurs called dromaeosaurids (DROM-ee-oh-SORE-ids). Speed, agility, good eyesight, and – above all – sharp weapons made them one of the deadliest groups of predators. Although their bodies look bird-like, they had powerful legs for running at high speeds, and stiff tails to help with balance as they kicked and slashed with their sickle-shaped toe claws.

FEARSOME TALONS

As part of a group called maniraptora ("hand-grabbers") dromaeosaurids had strong, grasping hands, often with fearsome finger talons. Scientists believe that, relative to their body weight, dromaeosaurids had the biggest brains of all the dinosaurs, and so were among the most intelligent.

"TERRIBLE CLAW"

Deinonychus (die-NON-ee-KUS) means "terrible claw" and its sickle claw was as sharp as a meat cleaver. Its eyes could look forward, giving binocular vision, so it could assess the distance of prey more accurately and judge the point at which it was close enough to kick, grab, or leap for an accurate attack. Its curved sawing teeth bit and tore flesh from the bones of its prey. A study of Deinonychus led scientists to believe it was probably warm-blooded, so its feather covering was necessary to maintain its temperature – unlike cold-blooded creatures, which did not need the insulation.

DINOSAUR DETECTIVES

Fossil footprints help scientists to work out how big a dinosaur was. Tracks are even more useful as they show how dinosaurs behaved. The distance between footprints shows how fast the animal was moving. Fossils showing a mix of large and small footprints indicate that the dinosaur lived in herds.

CAUGHT MID-BATTLE

The use of the sickle-shaped claw as a deadly weapon was proved by a fossil find: a Velociraptor's second toe claw was found attached to the ribs of a Protoceratops. The sheep-sized plant eater was clearly trying to fight off the Velociraptor when both died suddenly in mid-battle, perhaps in a landslide.

TIPTOE

Velociraptor (vel-OSS-ee-rap-tor) raised its second toe when it walked so the claw did not touch the ground. This was to prevent it from becoming blunt. When Velociraptor attacked, it used its powerful kick to stab the razor-sharp claw into its prey.

CARNOTAURUS

"FLESH-EATING BULL"

Carnotaurus (KAR-no-TORE-us) means "flesh-eating bull". With two horns and a powerful, bulky body, this theropod certainly had a bull-like appearance. It had a hunter's forward-facing vision and legs that could chase prey at high speed. Less powerful were its puzzlingly small arms, each with four fingers. It also had weak teeth and jaw muscles.

Carnotaurus didn't have a powerful bite (only 340 kg / 0.3 tons – much weaker than T. rex's 1,360 kg / 1.5 tons). However, it had the muscles to head-butt its prey. Its unusual skull was made up of separate moving parts, so it could absorb more pressure during head butts or bites.

SCENT OF FRESH MEAT

Carnotaurus probably followed its nose to find its prey. Its deep skull had an especially large hole in front of the eye sockets, suggesting that the dinosaur's sense of smell was above average for a hunter. It probably stalked its prey by following its scent.

HORN FIGHTS

Carnotaurus's horns stick out sideways just above the eyes, and may have been used in male-to-male fights. They may also have been used to help knock out its prey, or for display in the mating season. Its strong neck would have given Carnotaurus colossal power if it butted a rival. For extra protection in sparring or attacks, Carnotaurus had pebbly, lizard-like skin with larger lumps down its back.

VITAL STATISTICS

CARNOTAURUS

Meaning of name: Flesh-eating bull

Family: Abelisauridae

Period: Mid Cretaceous

Size: 3 m / 9.8 ft height; 7.5 m / 25 ft length

Weight: 1,000 kg / 1.1 tons

Diet: Meat

TROODON

NIGHT TRACKER

Troodon (TROH-oh-don) had a body that was similar in shape to an ostrich, yet unlike any ostrich living today, it was a killer. This meat-eater is estimated to have had more than 100 teeth, all sharp and triangular with serrated edges for cutting.

Troodon teeth have been found near fossils of baby hadrosaurs, suggesting they enjoyed tucking into vulnerable hatchlings. Troodon means "wounding tooth" and was named after a single pointed tooth from an early discovery.

BRAINY

Troodon had an unusually large brain compared to its body weight, making it one of the more intelligent dinosaurs.

KILLER TOES

Long legs meant a long stride, so Troodon could probably run fast. At the end of each second toe there was a curved claw, which could have done serious damage to any creature it was chasing.

GRABBING CLAWS

Troodon's clawed hands could meet palm to palm, so they could get a firm grasp on small living prey.

NIGHT VISION

Large, forward-facing eyes gave Troodon binocular vision and may also have enabled it to hunt in poor light, such as at dusk, or even at night like a cat. A pack of troodon would have been capable of bringing down prey much larger than themselves.

TROODON VERSUS DOMESTIC CAT

How do these night hunters measure up?

	TROODON:	DOMESTIC CAT
HEIGHT...	1 m / 40 in	0.20-0.25 m / 8-10 in
WEIGHT...	45 kg / 99 lb	3-4 kg / 7-9 lb
SPEED...	40 kph / 25 mph	48 kph / 30 mph
NUMBER OF TEETH...	100+	30
EYESIGHT...	Excellent	Excellent

TERRIFYING TEETH

Dinosaur teeth were harder than bone, so were more often preserved as fossils. Scientists can work out a great deal from fossilized teeth, such as what the dinosaurs ate.

MASSIVE EATER

Allosaurus, a 3-tonne (3.3 ton) predator that lived in Jurassic times, had teeth with serrated edges for sawing through flesh. The teeth were 5–10 cm (2–4 in) long and relatively small for a predator, but they were pointed and curved backward – perfect for tearing off giant chunks of its victims' flesh. Allosaurus bite marks have been found in the backbone of an Apatosaurus (a-PAT-oh-SORE-us), a huge sauropod, and the neck bone of the plated Stegosaurus (STE-go-SORE-us) – proof of the deadliness of its teeth. If any teeth broke off or were worn down, they were shed, and new teeth grew in their place, so the Allosaurus was never without its lethal bite.

FLESH SAWS

Some scientists believe that predators like Allosaurus would have used their teeth like a rasp, to strip off flesh from still-living prey. Rather than attacking it head-on and risking injury, they would instead wait for their victim to slowly bleed to death.

TYPES OF TEETH

We can identify plant-eaters from their peg-like teeth or sharp but toothless beaks, which were used for grazing. The meat- and fish-eaters had terrifying teeth – strong and sharp for grabbing and catching their prey, for tearing at flesh and crushing bone.

VENOMOUS BITE

Some scientists have suggested that Sinornithosaurus (SINE-or-nith-oh-SORE-us) used its curved, snake-like fangs to inject venom into its prey. This feathered, bird-like dinosaur, though no bigger than a turkey, may have killed prey much bigger than itself, by first subduing it with its venomous bite.

DINOSAUR DETECTIVES

We can discover how powerful a dinosaur's bite was from the size and shape of its tooth fossils, and from making reconstructions of its jaws to shows its muscles and their likely power. Tooth marks in a victim's fossils may be useful clues to bite strength, but they do not prove that the biter killed its victim as it may have already been dead and the dinosaur was feeding on its carcass.

BARYONYX

FISH HUNTER

Although slightly smaller than its famous relative, Spinosaurus, Baryonyx (baa-ree-ON-iks) was no less deadly. It is one of the few fish-hunting dinosaurs so far discovered, but had the lethal weapons necessary to ensure its success.

Some scientists suggest that although Baryonyx was a land animal, it swam in rivers and lakes, too, hunting from the surface of the water. It may also have caught fish from the shoreline, like a crocodile. It was thought to have eaten only fish until the bones of an Iguanodon (ig-WHA-no-don) were found in the stomach of one of its fossils. So it probably took every opportunity to grab any kind of meaty meal.

VITAL STATISTICS

BARYONYX

Meaning of name: Heavy claw

Family: Spinosauridae

Period: Early Cretaceous

Size: 2.5 m / 8 ft height; 10 m / 33 ft length

Weight: 1,800 kg / 2 tons

Diet: Fish and meat

A FULL STOMACH

Fossilized remains of fish scales, fish bones, and partially digested Iguanodon bones found in the stomach of a Baryonyx show its diet.

CAGE OF TEETH

Its 96 long, pointed teeth were designed for capturing and gripping fish. A dip in its lower jaw may have helped to keep a hold of any slippery, struggling fish, too.

FISH SNATCHER

Baryonyx had long crocodile-like jaws that it could dip into the water to snatch fish. Like a crocodile, it may have used the tip of its jaws to sense any movement in the water and so be able to open its mouth just in time to catch any passing prey.

HUGE CLAW

Baryonyx's name means "huge claw" and refers to the 0.3 m (1 ft) long claws on its thumbs. It may have used these like skewers or knives, to stab and tear the fish that it had caught, making it ready to eat. Its teeth were too spiked to do the job – designed to catch, not crush or chew.

PACKS AND FAMILIES

Predators did not always hunt or live alone. Some, such as Velociraptor, may have roamed around and hunted in packs.

STRENGTH IN NUMBERS

Protoceratops would have lived in large herds for protection. However, if a young, sick, or old animal became separated from the others, it could become a target for predators, such as these Velociraptors. The Protoceratops' horns and frill could perhaps have fended off a single attacker, but against a group it would have had little chance.

TEAMWORK

Working together, a pack of Velociraptors would have made short work of a lone Protoceratops. Like a modern pride of lions, the predators would have cooperated to bring down their prey. One would have attacked the horned head, while another went for the unguarded rear of the creature.

FAMILY PROTECTION

Even the most powerful dinosaurs, such as Allosaurus (shown here) were vulnerable to predators when young. So Allosaurus nested in groups, probably for shared protection. In one Allosaurus nesting site, scientists found fossil bones of different aged creatures, from hatchlings to elderly adults. There were no young adults, however, so perhaps they were thought strong enough to go off and fend for themselves. Fossil bones of hadrosaurs with Allosaurus bite marks were also found there, indicating they were the families' source of food.

DINOSAUR DETECTIVES

We know that a carnivorous dinosaur called Albertosaurus (al-BERT-o-SORE-us) moved around in packs because the fossil bones of 26 Albertosauruses were discovered in one area of Canada. The dinosaurs were of all different ages, from 2 to 23. Forty Allosaurus were also found in one area of Utah, USA. They may have died while trapped in mud — along with the dinosaurs they were hunting.

DINOSAUR DEFENDERS

An Ankylosaur swings its heavy tail club to defend itself against a group of hungry Albertosauruses.

The age of the dinosaurs was a violent time, with savage battles between hunting carnivores and defending herbivores. Just as meat-eating dinosaurs had killer features, plant eaters had defensive features, including protective plating, spikes, horns, and powerful, swinging tails.

Some dinosaurs sought safety in numbers by living in herds, just as modern-day grazing animals do. Patterned skin may have helped with camouflage, and the sheer size of some sauropods would have put off even the most aggressive hunters.

ARMS RACE

Throughout the long history of the dinosaurs, predators and prey were locked in an arms race, with species evolving ever-improving ways of attacking and defending. As carnivores became larger, stronger, and fiercer with longer teeth and more powerful claws, so herbivores evolved their own features to avoid becoming a meal. Skin grew thicker, bodies grew bigger, tails grew more powerful, and horns became longer and sharper. The result was some of the most fearsomely defended creatures ever to walk the planet.

WALKING TANK

The herbivorous Ankylosaurus (ANK-ill-oh-SORE-us) would probably have put up quite a fight against the aggressive hunter, Albertosaurus (al-BERT-oh-SORE-russ). Ankylosaurus was covered in a thick shield of bony knobs. Large plates protected its head and neck, and even its eyelids. Four horns at the back of its head warded off biting mouths. Its club-like tail was a defensive weapon that could be swung at an approaching predator. To get a chance of a decent bite, Albertosaurus would have had to turn Ankylosaurus over and attack it from underneath.

TRICERATOPS
HORN-FACED FIGHTER

Even the fearsome T. rex would have found the defensive systems of Triceratops (tri-SEH-ra-tops) difficult to penetrate. Triceratops was one of the huge, four-footed dinosaurs that grazed on plants in late Cretaceous times, and it had to defend itself against some of the most aggressive hunters that ever stalked the Earth.

Built like a giant rhino, Triceratops was the largest of the horned and frilled ceratopsians (seh-ra-TOPS-ee-ans).

THREE-HORNED FACE
Triceratops' name means "three-horned face". Its huge head was one-third of its body length. The two horns, one above each eye, were about 1 m (3 ft) long.

SPIKED NECKLACE
The neck plate, called a "frill", was huge and solid, and edged with knobs of bone for protection. The frill may have been patterned to attract a mate. It might have lowered its head to show off the frill – like a peacock displaying its feathers.

CRUSHING TEETH
Triceratops teeth were built for chomping through vegetation. Rather than chewing, it just crushed, then swallowed.

CHARGE!

If Triceratops sensed danger or competition from another male in the breeding season, it may have lowered its head like a rhino or bull and charged. With its truck-sized body weight behind it, the sharp horns would have been deadly weapons. Just the sight of a Triceratops' horns and huge frill might have been enough to scare off a predator.

TRICERATOPS VERSUS RHINOCEROS

	TRICERATOPS	RHINO
HEIGHT	3 m / 10 ft	1.5 m / 5 ft
LENGTH	8 m / 26 ft	4 m / 13 ft
WEIGHT	5,400–10,800 kg / 6–12 tons	3,600 kg / 4 tons
SPEED	Up to 26 kph / 16 mph	55 kph / 34 mph
NUMBER OF TEETH	400–800	24–34
HORNS	3 horns, 1 m / 3 ft	2 horns, the largest up to 1.5 m / 4.9 ft

FRIGHTENING FRILLS

A bizarre variety of aggressive-looking horns and strange neck plates, or frills, have been found on the heavily defended ceratopsians. A stampeding herd of Styracosaurus (sty-RAK-oh-SORE-us) or Centrosaurus (CEN-troh-SORE-us) would have scared off most predators. Another defensive tactic may have been to circle the aggressor and slowly close in.

Not all ceratopsian frills were large, so some scientists think they were not for protection but for show, and a way of recognizing members of the same herd. Brightly patterned frills would have made it easier to identify any competitors that were invading their patch. Other scientists believe that frills weren't used for show, but to help regulate the creatures' body temperatures. Of course it's possible that they had more than one use.

SPIKEY

Styracosaurus had a horrifying array of spikes and horns. As well as a massive nose horn, it had up to eight spikes sticking out from its neck frill, and a horn protruding from each cheek. There's some evidence that young Styracosaurus had two further horns, one above each eye, which fell off when they were adults.

LIGHTWEIGHT MONSTER

Ceratopsian neck frills must have been heavy, but Centrosaurus's had two big holes in the bony structure covered by skin, making it lighter. Moving to get away was perhaps more important for this dinosaur as two of its horns look rather useless – they point down rather than out. However, the long nose horn could have done some damage in a head-butting battle. The vulnerability of the holey frill suggests that it was for display and to deter, rather than to protect. Face-on, the frill would have made Centrosaurus's head look bigger than it really was to advancing hunters.

DINOSAUR DETECTIVES

Dinosaur hunters do most of their work with fossilized bones, though occasionally other parts are found. This is a skin impression of a ceratopsian. It shows that the skin was made up of small plates, similar to those on a crocodile.

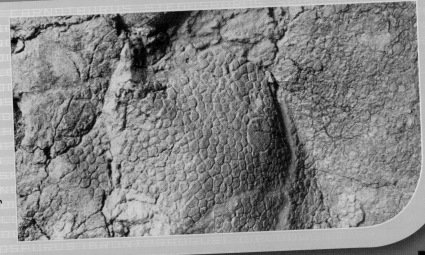

PACHYCEPHALOSAURIDS

BUTTING BONEHEADS

The two-legged, plant-eating pachycephalosaurids (PACK-ee-SEF-ah-low-SORE-ids) are sometimes nicknamed "boneheads". It's possible they may have head-butted each other like goats in fights over territory or mates. This strange tactic was possible because they had a layer of solid, thick bone over the top of their heads, like crash helmets.

Some scientists argue that the domes must have been for display, not protection, as they would not have been strong enough to withstand being rammed into another bony head or body. The best known of the boneheads from fossil evidence is Stegoceras (ste-GOS-er-as).

HEAD BUTTER

Stegoceras may have used their heads to hit their opponents sideways rather than full-on, so as to avoid serious injury.

BARBED TIARA

A frill of knobs and horns surrounded the domed head like a crown. This might have been for show or for extra protection, or to cause more damage when the creature swiped its head at the enemy.

SHOCK ABSORBER

Scientists have calculated that Stegoceras's backbone and neck were strong enough to take the shock of a collision if it rammed its head into an attacker.

THICK HEAD

Pachycephalosaurus (PACK-ee-SEF-ah-low-SORE-us) means "thick-headed lizard", and it is well named – its dome was about 20 cm (8 in) thick. Standing 6 m (20 ft) tall, it was a giant amongst the pachycephalosaurids. Its three types of teeth suggest it probably fed on plants, fruit, and insects.

DINOSAUR DETECTIVES

A tall horn-like crown may have grown upwards from the dome on pachycephalosaurids like an odd sort of wizard's hat. Evidence of blood vessels in the bony domes suggest this possibility. If so, it was probably there for display.

STEGOSAURUS

SAVAGE SPIKES

Stegosaurus (STE-go-SORE-us), a herbivorous, coach-sized dinosaur, had some incredible defensive features to aid its survival. And it needed them, because it lived among some of the biggest and most dangerous hunters of Jurassic times, including Allosaurus (AL-oh-SORE-us) and Ceratosaurus (Keh-RAT-oh-SORE-us).

ROOF LIZARD
Stegosaurus's name means "roof lizard" and this refers to its back plates. It had 17 plates in all, and the biggest was about 76 cm (2.5 ft) tall. The plates may have become brighter in the mating season to attract mates.

NECK STUDS
The neck and throat are among the most vulnerable parts of the body when it comes to a deadly bite. Stegosaurus had bony studs to protect this area.

STING IN ITS TAIL
Two pairs of thorn-like spikes stuck out sideways from the end of its tail – a dangerous defensive weapon that it could swing in the direction of any hunter that got too close.

BODY STUDS

Stegosaurus is well known for the plate-like spikes that run down its back. But it also had body studs for extra protection. Its back legs were longer than its front legs, which meant it could turn quite quickly and thwack its spiky tail at an unwelcome creature.

TINY BRAIN

Stegosaurus's brain was only the size of a modern dog's, making it the smallest brain compared to body size of any dinosaur. But what it lacked in smarts, it made up for in other ways. Scientists believe it had cheeks – a relatively rare feature in dinosaurs – helping this plant-eater to chew its food properly.

BACK PLATE MYSTERY

There is some evidence that the bases of the back plates were muscular, and Stegosaurus could twist them in the direction of predators. No one knows for sure whether the plates were covered in horn and were for protection, or covered in skin and used to regulate Stegosaurus's temperature. If they were covered in skin, blood in the plates would have heated up in the sun, then spread to the rest of the body when the warm sunshine disappeared later in the day. If the dinosaur was too hot, the plates could have been used to release excess body heat.

VITAL STATISTICS

STEGOSAURUS

Meaning of name:
Roof lizard

Family: Stegosauridae

Period: Late Jurassic

Size: 4 m / 14 ft height;
9 m / 30 ft length

Weight: 1,800 kg / 2 tons

Diet: Plants

ANKYLOSAURS

DEFENSIVE DEMONS

Ankylosaurs (ang-KEY-loh-sores) were bulky herbivores boasting an awesome array of defensive spikes, plates, and tail clubs. They all had thick plating over their backs and scary-looking spikes that stuck out from the sides of their bodies.

MENACING MACE

Like a knight's mace, the bony knob at the end of Ankylosaurus's tail could be swung at threatening carnivores. Long bones and powerful muscles in its tail gave it devastating power. Evidence suggests that with a swing of this tail, Ankylosaurus could have smashed the bones of any attacking dinosaur.

PROTECTIVE PLATING

Plating would have protected its back, neck, and shoulders. Spiky knobs would have made it difficult for an aggressor to get close enough to flip the heavy monster over and attack its softer underbelly.

BONY EYELIDS

Even Ankylosaurus's eyes were shielded. Its eyelids, as well as the rest of its head, were protected by a helmet of fused bony plates (hence its name, which means "fused lizard").

DEADLY CLUBS

The early Cretaceous ankylosaurs, like Gastonia (gas-TOE-nee-ah), were small. But by late Cretaceous times, ankylosaurs faced threats from powerful carnivores such as Albertosaurus. They became larger and heavier, with defensive plating and deadly clubs at the ends of their tails.

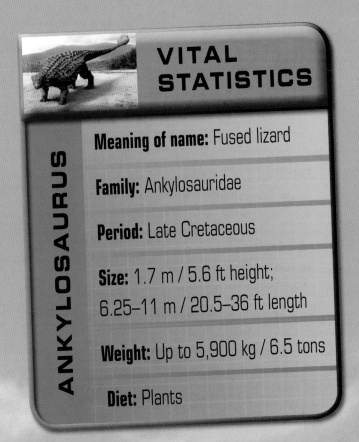

VITAL STATISTICS

ANKYLOSAURUS

Meaning of name: Fused lizard

Family: Ankylosauridae

Period: Late Cretaceous

Size: 1.7 m / 5.6 ft height; 6.25–11 m / 20.5–36 ft length

Weight: Up to 5,900 kg / 6.5 tons

Diet: Plants

BLADED TAIL

Gastonia may have been tormented by the agile, sharp-clawed hunter Utahraptor (YOO-ta-RAP-tor), as they lived in the same part of North America. But Gastonia had thick plating protecting its neck, back, and tail. And it had a set of blade-like spikes on its tail that would have cut through the air like a knife and done serious damage to any Utahraptor that got too close.

HADROSAURS

DEAFENING DUCKBILLS

Hadrosaurs (HA-dro-sores) were duck-billed dinosaurs with huge, hollow crests on their heads. Different types had differently shaped crests, and some looked very bizarre. It seems likely that they were used as an alarm.

Many scientists think the crests would have been used to make mating calls, to attract other hadrosaurs during the mating season. By varying the amount of air blown through the hollow tubes in its crest, a hadrosaur could raise or lower the volume of the call.

WARNING!

The honking alarm call of Parasaurolophus (PAH-ra-sore-OLL-oh-fuss) would alert others in its herd to flee or gather for protection. Although they spent most of their time on four legs, they could run on two legs for short periods when pursued by predators.

SHOW-OFF

The curved head crest may have been brightly marked, either to warn off attackers or to attract a mate. Males and females probably had different sized crests, with the largest on the males.

SLIPPING THROUGH THE FORESTS

By keeping its head raised, the back of Parasaurolophus's crest might have rested on its back, creating a smooth, streamlined shape. This would have helped it pass through thick undergrowth quickly and quietly. Parasaurolophus would have found greater safety in a herd, and even more so if they could move without making too much noise.

HELMET LIZARD

The crest of Corythosaurus (core-ith-oh-SORE-us) was shaped like half a plate. This accounts for its name, which means "Corinthian helmet lizard". Its crest looks a bit like the helmet worn by the ancient Greeks of Corinth. Corythosaurus also had protective shielding under its body in the form of three rows of scales. These may have been to defend against injury from prickly plants in the undergrowth.

DINOSAUR DETECTIVES

The set of curved hollow tubes in the crest of Parasaurolophus were connected to the nostrils. By studying the flow of air through these tubes, scientists have worked out that Parasauralophus could have made a loud and deep trumpeting noise when it snorted through its nose. The hollow tubes probably acted as resonators, just as the empty body of a guitar increases the loudness of the strings.

SAUROPODS

TAIL-THRASHING TITANS

With legs as big as tree trunks, size was the sauropods' most important means of protection. A titanosaur like Ampelosaurus (AM-pel-oh-SORE-us) was four times heavier than a predator like Tarascosaurus (ta-RASS-koh-SORE-us). But if hungry, a killer carnivore might still risk an attack, hoping to achieve a fatal bite. Its reward would be a meal that lasted several days.

BULLYING BULK

A predator would normally prefer to stalk weak prey, such as young or smaller dinosaurs, or even hatchlings and eggs, rather than risk being knocked over by the weight of a sauropod. But if hungry enough, a 9-m (30-ft) long Tarascosaurus might well take on an Ampelosaurus, even though it was massively bigger at 15 m (50 ft) long, and well defended.

WHIP AND STABILISER

Ampelosaurus's tail could lash out at a pursuer, as well act as a counterbalance to its weight if it chose to rise up on its hind legs to defend itself.

LIGHT PROTECTION

Unlike the earlier, heavily plated sauropods, Ampelosaurus had light shielding. The bony lumps under its skin provided some protection against the mouths of hungry attackers.

SWUNG LIKE A WHIP

Around 27 m (90 ft) long and weighing up to 18 tonnes (20 tons), the sauropod Diplodocus (DIP-low-DOH-kus) had a very long, 14-m (46-ft) tail that it could have swung like a rope to thrash attackers. Two sets of bones under its tail made it a powerful weapon. When it lashed out with this massive whip, it probably made an intimidating cracking sound.

DINOSAUR DETECTIVES

We know that Diplodocus's tail was not so heavy that it had to be dragged along the ground, because there are no tail tracks where Diplodocus footprints have been discovered.

PATTERNS AND FEATHERS

For a long time scientists thought that dinosaurs were rather drab and dull looking. However, recent discoveries have changed their minds. Now they believe that many species had patterned skin or brightly shaded feathers.

The patterns would have helped to camouflage the dinosaurs, allowing predators to sneak up on prey – and prey to stay hidden from predators.

TONES AND SHADES

We don't know the exact tones or shades of any dinosaur skin, as none of the pigments have survived in fossils. They may have been bright for display, to attract a mate or warn off a rival.

MUMMIFIED DUCKBILL

Some skin as well as bones were preserved in a mummified duckbill. The preserved skin showed striped patterns – the first evidence of what a dinosaur skin really looked like and how it may have been camouflaged like a modern-day reptile.

WHO WAS IT HIDING FROM?

The hadrosaurs, like the one shown here, were stalked by some of the most dangerous meat-eaters, including the terrifying Tyrannosaurus rex.

FIRST FEATHERS

In 1996, a spectacular discovery was made in a quarry in China: the first dinosaur fossil to show evidence of a feathery covering. The dinosaur was Sinosauropteryx (SIGH-no-sore-OP-ter-ix), a small meat-eater of the early Cretaceous. The feathers may have had markings for camouflage or display. By studying preserved pigment cells, scientists worked out that it had rings of orange and white feathers alternating down its long tail, like a tabby cat. Pigments on later dino-bird feathers reveal a range of dark shadings that would have made them very bright.

 ## DINOSAUR DETECTIVES

Well-preserved fossil feathers are a rare find, but some from Anchiornis (ANN-chee-OR-niss), a bird-like dinosaur, were discovered and studied. Through detailed analysis scientists worked out that its body feathers were black, white, and dullish silver, and its head crest was red.

HERDING HEAVIES

There is strength in numbers, and just as modern-day animals gather together to graze, migrate, and mate, dinosaurs such as Protoceratops (pro-toe-SER-ah-tops) and Triceratops would have, too. In a group there would have been more watchful eyes and listening ears. If one sensed danger it would run, and the others would follow.

Experts used to think the biggest plant-eating dinosaurs lived alone, especially if they had powerful defensive shielding like Triceratops. But evidence has revealed that even these mighty beasts roamed in herds. Areas where lots of bones are found together are the best indication of herds. In one part of Alberta, Canada, hundreds of bones of Centrosaurus were found together – evidence of a huge herd, which probably drowned in a flood after a storm.

TITANOSAUR TEENS

The fossils of three young titanosaurs were found huddled together. They might have died in a flood and were too young and weak to escape with the adults. It is likely that young titanosaurs would have been protected in a herd. A vulnerable baby would be less likely to be picked off by a predator if surrounded by a mass of giant adults.

SHIELDED SHEEP

Protoceratops was only the size of sheep and its weak neck plate was just for display. The dinosaurs probably moved in herds because they would have struggled to defend themselves as individuals. We know they were vulnerable because one Protoceratops fossil was found with a Velociraptor (vel-OSS-ih-rap-tore) skeleton wrapped around it, as if they both died in the midst of battle.

WALL OF HORNS

Like musk ox and other modern-day horned creatures, Triceratops could have created a defensive wall by forming a line or circle and facing their attacker together. This would have been enough to intimidate any predator.

RECORD-BREAKERS

The biggest dinosaurs were the titanosaurs (tie-TAN-oh-sores). These colossal sauropods would make any land animal alive today look small. Some were taller than a five-floor building, the length of at least three buses, and the weight of 17 African elephants.

The biggest of the carnivorous dinosaurs, like Giganotosaurus (jig-an-OH-toe-SORE-us), were still smaller than the plant-eating sauropods. But these ferocious hunting machines were record-breakers in other ways, having the biggest teeth and the most powerful bites. They were capable of killing dinosaurs far larger than themselves.

RECORD-BREAKING WEAPONS

Dinosaurs had some of the sharpest teeth, the longest claws, the most aggressive tails, and the deadliest kicks known to nature. Teeth were the biggest killers: Tyrannosaurus rex boasted teeth that were up to 23 cm (9 in) long; Giganotosaurus teeth were only a little shorter, at 20 cm (8 in).

A pair of hungry giganotosaurs would have been a match even for a record-breaking titanosaur.

TITANS

The titanosaurs, the tallest, longest, and heaviest dinosaurs to walk the Earth, were named after the Titans, the powerful gods of ancient Greece. One was Antarctosaurus (an-TARC-toe-SORE-us), which had an estimated length of up to 30 m (98 ft). As a grazer, it would have been a gentle giant, eating plants all day – unless attacked!

GIGANOTOSAURUS: FEROCIOUS GIANT

Because of its size, Giganotosaurus must have had a huge appetite, and hunger would have overcome any fear of attacking a titanosaur. A battle between these two vast creatures would have been an awesome sight. The Giganotosaurus would have charged at its prey and attempted a fatal bite while avoiding being swept away by the titanosaur's whip-like tail.

THE TITANOSAURS
THE HEAVYWEIGHTS

The super heavyweights of the dinosaur world were the giant sauropods, the titanosaurs. Weighing in at 100 tonnes (100 tons), their long necks and tails gave them record-breaking lengths too.

DOUBLE WINNER

Argentinosaurus (ARE-jen-teen-oh-SORE-us) became a double record holder as the heaviest (80–100 tonnes or 88–110 tons) and the longest (up to 35 m, or 115 ft) of all the dinosaurs, after a ranger found a fossil from its leg in 1987. The leg was so big, the ranger thought it was part of a tree. Computers have been used to estimate how such a heavy creature could move, and the answer is very slowly – only 8 kph (5 mph), even with its long legs.

Before its fossil was lost, the record-holder for size and weight was thought to be Amphicoelias (am-fih-SEAL-ee-us). The fossil, a single vertebra of truly massive proportions, suggested an animal 60 m (200 ft) long and weighing more than 125 tonnes (138 tons).

SHIELDED TITANS

Some of the titanosaurs, like Saltasaurus (SALT-a-SORE-us), were heavy, at around 10 tonnes (11 tons), but not big enough for their size to protect them. Instead, hard, bony plates and bumps covered Saltasaurus's back to deter biting hunters.

ARGENTINOSAURUS VERSUS AFRICAN ELEPHANT

	ARGENTINOSAURUS	AFRICAN ELEPHANT
LENGTH	35 m / 115 ft	7.5 m / 25 ft
HEIGHT	21 m / 70 ft	4 m / 13 ft
WEIGHT	99, 790 kg / 110 tons	6,350 kg / 7 tons
SPEED	8 kph / 5 mph	Up to 40 kph / 25 mph
FOOD	Plants	Plants

SMALLEST DINOSAURS

Not all dinosaurs were heavyweight giants. Many in Jurassic and Cretaceous times were only as high as a human's waist – some barely knee-high. But even the smallest were aggressive little hunters with jaws full of sharp, cutting teeth.

Compsognathus (KOMP-sog-NATH-us) holds the record for the smallest dinosaur found without feathers. Even smaller was the feathered Microraptor (MIKE-row-RAP-tor), which holds the record for the tiniest bird-like dinosaur. They would have been able to run fast in search of their prey, snapping up small reptiles, insects, or fish.

STEADY AS SHE GOES
A long tail helped Compsognathus with its balance as it raced along after its prey. Its long legs suggest that it was a speedy runner.

A TASTE FOR LIZARDS
Smaller than some turkeys, Compsognathus was about 1 m (3 ft) tall and would have eaten small creatures and insects. The fossil of an unlucky lizard was found in the stomach of a fossilized Compsognathus – its last meal before it died.

PRETTY JAWS
Compsognathus means "dainty jaws" but they would not have looked so pretty to its prey. Its teeth were sharp at the front and flatter but serrated at the back.

THE PLUNDERER

Microraptor means "small plunderer", and this crow-sized dinosaur is the smallest feathered, bird-like dinosaur yet discovered, with a length of just 40 cm (16 in). It may have used its feathered limbs to glide from tree to tree, but it was not built for proper flight.

DINOSAUR DETECTIVES

Is it tiny or just young? This is the question scientists must ask themselves when they examine small dinosaur remains. The smallest skeleton yet found was Mussaurus (moo-SORE-us), at 37 cm (14.5 in) long, but it was later revealed to be a hatchling and not fully grown.

SPINOSAURUS

The prize for biggest hunter goes to this mythical-looking monster, which appears to have the head of a crocodile and the body of a dragon. It was one of the most fantastical of all dinosaurs, and its name, Spinosaurus (SPINE-oh-SORE-us), means "spined lizard".

DON'T HOLD YOUR BREATH

Spinosaurus didn't have to hold its breath while it pushed its hungry mouth into the water. Its nostrils were high up on its head, so they were well out of the water for easy breathing.

SKIN AND SPINES

Spinosaurus's tremendous sail was made up of long backbone spines, with skin stretched across. It was used either to terrorize other dinosaurs or to control its body heat, or perhaps both.

TRAP

Like other spinosaurids, Spinosaurus's teeth were different from other meat-eating giants. Not only did they have more teeth, but they were smaller and straighter, with a hooked set at the front – ideal for trapping and grasping slippery fish.

FILM STAR

Spinosaurus became famous when it was featured in the film *Jurassic Park III*. These narrow-jawed monsters were even bigger than Giganotosaurus and Tyrannosaurus rex. It had different eating habits from those meat-eaters as well, preferring to hunt in rivers and lakes and catch fish. Second prize for biggest hunter goes to Carcharodontosaurus (kar-KAR-oh-don-toe-sore-us) – another huge predator.

VITAL STATISTICS

SPINOSAURUS

Meaning of name: Spined lizard

Family: Spinosauridae

Period: Early Cretaceous

Size: 5 m / 16 ft height; 18 m / 59 ft length

Weight: Possibly up to 20,000 kg / 22 tons

Diet: Fish and perhaps meat

RUNNER-UP

Carcharodontosaurus was a massive meat-eater, 15 m (49 ft) long, and had one of the biggest skulls ever discovered (1.53 m or 5 ft, in length). Although its skull was longer than a T. rex's, it had a much smaller brain cavity, so perhaps it wasn't so bright. It had huge curved and serrated meat-eating teeth that were up to 20 cm (8 in) long.

DEADLIEST DINOSAUR

Tyrannosaurus rex is often described as the deadliest dinosaur. Its skeleton, especially its jaws and teeth, is evidence of its incredible ferocity, power, and ability to kill. For more than 100 years, it also held the record for the biggest meat-eater.

BONE CRUSHERS

Tyrannosaurus had a bite three times more powerful than a Giganotosaurus. It could crush bone and puncture the toughest of skins. Its backward-slanting teeth made it virtually impossible for its victims to escape once they had been bitten.

TAIL BALANCE

The huge, heavy tail kept its body upright, and helped keep it balanced as it swung its head and jaws at its victim.

BATTERING RAM

Tyrannosaurus rex could have used its weight to push over or crush smaller prey. The powerful legs held up its giant body, but because of its size it probably could not run very fast. As a top killer, it would have faced few dangers it needed to run from, although it is possible that these monsters sometimes attacked each other.

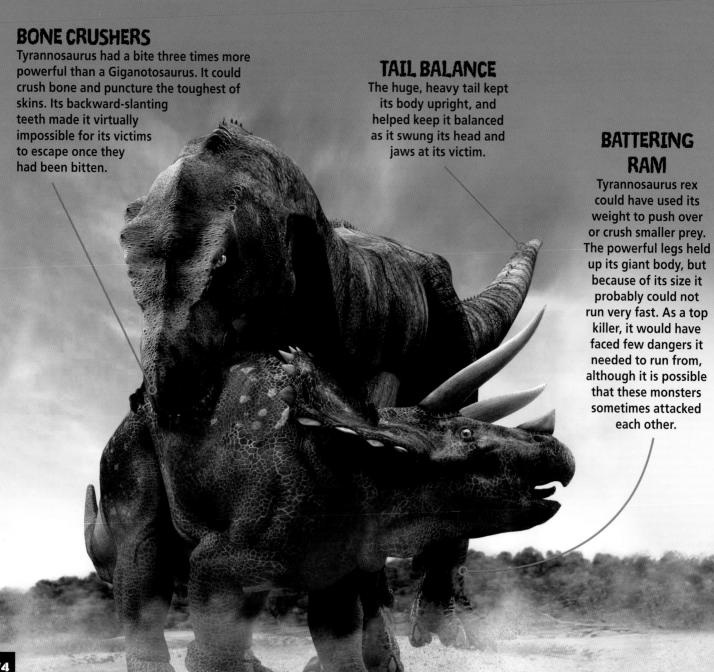

FANGS A LOT

Although we do not know if it had the sharpest of teeth, Tyrannosaurus rex does hold the record for the biggest dinosaur teeth. Scientists have also discovered that it had the most powerful bite of any land creature known.

DINOSAUR DETECTIVES

Body-Builder

By putting fossil skeletons together, it is possible to work out where T. rex's muscles would have been attached. The length of its bones and its build give clues to the strength and size of the muscles that this hunter would have needed to track its food and kill. The bones themselves tell us how it must have towered over many other dinosaurs of the time.

Power Bite

How do we know that T. rex had such a powerful bite? By scanning a skull it is possible to make a computer model of the dinosaur's jaws and muscles. The computer then works out the power of its bite when the muscles are pulled tight. The force of its upper and lower back teeth hitting each other was measured at between 3 and 6 tonnes (3–6 tons). By way of contrast, a human's bite force is just 110–130 kg (240–290 lbs).

SKYSCRAPERS

The tallest dinosaur was Sauroposeidon (SORE-oh-po-SIDE-on), which means "lizard of Poseidon". Poseidon was the Greek god of the sea and earthquakes, and Sauroposeidon does look like a monster from a myth. Yet it lived for real, grazing on tall-growing plants of the Cretaceous era.

Some of the tallest and longest dinosaurs were sauropods. They were herbivores who moved around on four legs and used their necks to reach the highest leaves. They may also have used them to reach for plants in marshy areas while keeping their feet safely on solid ground. Diplodocid (DIP-low-DOE-sid) sauropods, such as Supersaurus (SUE-per-SORE-us), had the longest necks of all.

STILT WALKER

Sauroposeidon walked on four legs, the front two longer than the back. When the fossilized neck bones of this creature were first discovered, they were thought to be prehistoric tree trunks and not bones at all, because they were so big. Scientists think that this giant stretched up to 17 m (56 ft) tall – higher than a five-floor building. The neck bones were filled with tiny holes to make them lighter. Without these holes, the neck and head may have been impossible to lift.

SUPER-NECK

Supersaurus (which means "super lizard") is a contender for the longest-neck record, but we cannot be certain because very few Supersaurus fossils have been found. However, by studying similar dinosaurs, and the neck fossils that have been discovered, scientists estimate that its neck was longer than a bus (14 m, or 46 ft). Like other sauropods, it had a small head, which means its brain was relatively small, so it would not have been the brightest of dinosaurs. Its long, thin tail could have been used like a whip to keep predators at bay. A strong flick might have caused serious damage, or at least given an attacker a nasty surprise.

SAUROPOSEIDON VERSUS GIRAFFE

	SAUROPOSEIDON	GIRAFFE
LENGTH	34 m / 112 ft	4.7 m / 15 ft
HEIGHT	17 m / 56 ft	6 m / 20 ft
WEIGHT	54,000 kg / 60 tons	1,600 kg / 3,524 lb
SPEED	8 kph / 5 mph	Up to 60 kph / 37 mph
FOOD	Plants	Plants

DINOSAUR EGG RECORDS

Most dinosaurs, from the sauropod giants like Brachiosaurus (BRAK-ee-oh-SORE-us) to the killer theropods like Tyrannosaurus rex, began their lives as small and vulnerable hatchlings emerging from eggs. If not fiercely guarded, the young dinosaurs could have been snatched up as an easy meal.

Even the largest dinosaurs came from surprisingly small eggs. Theropod eggs were only 10–15 cm (4–6 in) long, while the smallest fossilized dinosaur eggs would easily fit into the palm of a hand, at just 6.5 cm (2.5 in) long.

FOOTBALL-SIZE EGGS

Not much is known about the titanosaur Hypselosaurus (hip-SELL-oh-SORE-us), but the eggs found alongside its fossilized remains are record-breakers: they were the first dinosaur eggs to be found, and are also among the biggest eggs ever discovered. At 30 cm (1 ft) in length, they are the size of footballs. Scientists believe that dinosaur hatchlings must have grown very quickly to reach the giant sizes they became as adults, and also that they may have continued to grow throughout their lives, just as some modern-day reptiles do.

CRUEL WORLD

Mother dinosaurs laid between 3 and 20 eggs in one go. Many eggs and young dinosaurs would have been gobbled up by passing predators.

EGG HUNT

Dinosaur eggs are rare. They are most often found on ancient floodplains and sand dunes. The biggest ever deposit of dinosaur eggs was found on an ancient beach in northern Spain. It contained around 300,000 eggs. Very occasionally, dinosaur embryos are found inside the eggs.

EGGS ON THE RUN

Some of the biggest eggs were laid by the sauropod Apatosaurus. The mothers probably laid their eggs as they walked along, and didn't bother to build nests or look after the young hatchlings. Like all sauropod eggs, Apatosaurus eggs were somewhat spherical. Theropod eggs were more elongated.

DINOSAUR EGGS VERSUS OSTRICH EGGS

	HYPSELOSAURUS EGG	OSTRICH EGG
LENGTH	30 cm / 1 ft	15 cm / 5.9 in
WIDTH	25 cm / 10 in	13 cm / 5.1 in
VOLUME	2 l / 0.5 gallons	1.4 l / 0.35 gallons
WEIGHT	7 kg / 15.5 lb	1.4 kg / 3.1 lb

FASTEST DINOSAURS

On the plains of Cretaceous-era North America, smaller dinosaurs faced deadly dangers in the form of killers like Albertosaurus (al-BERT-oh-SORE-us). Panic-stricken at the sight of a predator, their only means of escape was running. The fastest were the most likely to survive, and there were none faster than the 'ostrich dinosaurs'.

The group of theropods known as 'ostrich dinosaurs' were ornithomimosaurs (or-NITH-oh-MIM-oh-sores), which means 'bird-mimic dinosaurs'. The fastest of all were Dromiceiomimus (dro-MI-see-oh-MEEM-us) and Struthiomimus (STRUTH-ee-oh-MEEM-us), who were astoundingly quick.

INSECT EATER?

Dromiceiomimus had a toothless bird-like beak and a weak jaw, suggesting it didn't attempt to catch large living creatures. However, it may have caught insects or lizards to top up its plant diet.

OSTRICH LEGS

Dromiceiomimus's body doesn't look much like an ostrich, but its slim legs, with long shins, gave it an ostrich-style speed. It ran at up to 80 kph (50 mph) – as fast as a cruising car.

SPRINTERS' FEET

Just as sprinters need a good tread on their shoes to stop them from slipping, this dinosaur used its three toe claws for extra grip.

STREAMLINED

Struthiomimus was another North American ostrich dinosaur. At about 1.8 m (6 ft) tall, it was a similar size to Dromiceiomimus. Its body had a streamlined shape, allowing it to run fast, and may have been covered in feathers. The tail helped to keep it balanced as it ran. Its little arms and three-clawed hands would only have been strong enough to pull down branches or poke at insect nests.

DINOSAUR DETECTIVES

Tracks made by dinosaurs are clues to how fast they ran. Their size and shape can be compared with those of similar creatures living today, such as the emus and ostriches, to work out their style of running and their speed.

LONGEST CLAWS

Among the most lethal dinosaur weapons are the claws. Therizinosaurus (THER-ih-ZINE-oh-SORE-us) had incredible claws on its forearms, the longest of any dinosaur. Utahraptor was the largest of the killer raptors and takes the record for the biggest toe-claws of the group.

Utahraptor's sharp, curved claws would have been fearsome weapons when both attacking and defending. However, Therizinosaurus's massive hand-claws would not have been used to attack prey, because it is thought that this bizarre-looking giant was a plant-eater.

SCYTHE CLAWS

The claws on Therizinosaurus (which means 'scythe lizard') were 58 cm (23 in) long. Their creepy three-fingered hands were at the end of arms that stretched to an incredible 2.45 m (8 ft). The claws may have been used to pull down branches to eat leaves, to warn off rivals or to defend it from hunters.

VITAL STATISTICS

THERIZINOSAURUS

Meaning of name: Scythe lizard

Family: Therizinosauridae

Period: Late Cretaceous

Size: 10 m / 33 ft length

Weight: Possibly up to 2,700 kg / 5,990 lb

Diet: Plants

TERRIFYING TOES

With a length of 7.6 m (25 ft), Utahraptor (YOO-ta-RAP-tor) was probably the biggest of the rampaging raptors. The lethal sickle-shaped claws on its second toes could have been up to 24 cm (9.4 in) long – a raptor record-breaker. The claws could have been used to bring down hadrosaurs or smaller sauropods with a skin-ripping kick. "Raptor" means "snatcher", and Utahraptor's grasping fingers would have clung like a leech to its victims.

TOUGH AS TANKS

PROTECTION

In 2003, a giant dinosaur skull was discovered in Mexico with the most awesome horns ever seen. Large horns had been seen before, on dinosaurs like Triceratops, but those on Coahuilaceratops (koh-WHE-lah-SEH-ra-tops) were record-breakers.

Coahuilaceratops's giant skull was 1.8 m (6 ft) long with horns that grew from just above the eyes. These horns could be up to 1.2 m (4 ft) in length. The dinosaur had a thick, strong neck to support the weight of the horns.

HORRIFIC HORNS

Ceratopsid (SEH-rah-TOP-sid) dinosaurs like Coahuilaceratops were herbivores. Their horns were for protection – to ward off predators and rival males - and probably to attract mates. Duels fought between pairs of Coahuilaceratops may well have ended in serious injury and maybe even death for at least one of the contestants.

PLATED PLANT-EATER

The most heavily protected dinosaur was undoubtedly Ankylosaurus. A late Cretaceous herbivore, it had heavy shielding made up of bony plates with raised bumps and spikes, which made it difficult for hunters to get a hold of it with their teeth. Thick plates protected the head, and four sharp horns stuck out at the back. The heavy knob on the end of its tail could crack bones when swung at its attackers.

COAHUILACERATOPS VERSUS RHINO

	COAHUILACERATOPS	RHINO
LENGTH	6.7 m / 22 ft	4 m / 13 ft
HEIGHT	1.8–2.1 m / 6–7 ft	1.5 m / 5 ft
WEIGHT	3,630 kg / 8,000 lb	3,600 kg / 7,900 lb
HORNS	Two	Two
HORN LENGTH	Up to 1.3 m / 4.25 ft	Up to 1.5 m / 4.9 ft

SAVAGE SKIES

While the dinosaurs ruled the land, the pterosaurs (TEH-roe-sores) were the tyrants of the sky. These powerful reptiles flew over the sea, coasts, and sometimes inland, snapping up insects, grabbing live fish, or tearing at carrion.

Some had strong toothless beaks, while others had needle-sharp teeth. They appeared around 200 million years ago and were at their peak in late Jurassic times, ranging from the size of tiny birds to monsters as big as a light aircraft. Swooping and gliding, pterosaurs could dive for fish in the sea or soar above the land, safe from the hungry jaws of the dinosaurs. Pterosaurs are traditionally divided into two types – pterodactyls (TEH-roe-DACK-tills) and rhamphorhynchoids (ram-foe-RINK-oids).

Winged pterosaurs soar above the Jurassic coast out of reach of the dinosaurs below.

WINGED WONDERS

Pterosaur means "winged lizard". Each wing of these reptiles was made of a leathery, elastic membrane, or skin. The membrane stretched from the body, across to a super-long fourth finger. The other fingers were clawed. The wing was thin but strong for flying, and did not tear easily.

NEEDLE-TOOTHED TERRORS

Rhamphorhynchus (ram-foe-RINK-us) had long fangs, a pointed beak, and a 1.8-m (6-ft) wide wingspan for stability – perfect for a fish hunter. With its wide wings it could fly low over the sea or lakes, using its sharp eyes to seek food.

FISH BASKET

There may have been a pouch in its throat, like a pelican's, so that it could catch several fish in one go.

DIAMOND RUDDER

The long tail had a diamond-shaped flap at the end, which probably helped steer it through the air, like a boat's rudder.

BEAK SNOUT

Rhamphorhynchus means "beak snout". Its protruding beak held 34 needle-sharp teeth (ten pairs at the top and seven below). They stuck out to the side and at the front – like a spiked cage that even slippery fish could not escape.

Its hunting method may have been to dip its toothy beak underwater, open its mouth, and snatch its prey. Some scientists think it may have caught several fish at once using a skimming technique – dragging its open beak along like an underwater plough. Its name gives away which of the two groups of pterosaurs it belongs to: it's a rhamphorhynchoid, not a pterodactyl. Rhamphorhynchoids had longer tails than pterodactyls.

FANG FACE

Eudimorphodon (YOU-die-MORE-fo-don), another rhamphorhynchoid, had more than 100 teeth, and some of its teeth had more than one point. This mass of sharp teeth was deadly for any fish it caught, and allowed no escape. Its long, curled toe-claws could grasp onto trees or cliff-tops. From these lookout places it could easily take off. Eudimorphodon is one of the earliest pterosaurs.

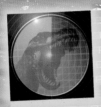

FLYING MONSTER DETECTIVES

How do we know what pterosaurs ate? The type of teeth are a clue, but the best evidence is the creatures' fossilized stomach contents, such as the fish scales found in the stomach of a Eudimorphodon.

PTERANODONS
AWESOME AXE-HEADS

With a wingspan three times bigger than a golden eagle, and a pointed head longer than its own body, Pteranodon (teh-RAN-oh-don) was an awesome pterosaur. These monsters probably soared over coastlines, diving to snap up fish, squid, and other Late Cretaceous creatures from the sea.

Although its jaws were toothless, they were powerful. Some Pteranodons had a large, backward-pointing head crest, giving them an aggressive, pickaxe-shaped profile. Like all pterodactyls, Pteranodon lacked a tail, so the crest may have acted as a rudder, helping it to turn as it swooped through the sky.

SHOW-OFFS

Pteranodon is famous for its crest. Fossils show that the crests varied in size, and some were quite small. This suggests that rather than helping with flight, they may have been used by the males to attract mates. If that is the case, then it's likely that the crests were brightly patterned.

BEASTLY BEAK

Pteranodon's beak was 1.2 m (4 ft) in length – longer than its own body. Its shape allowed it to dip down deep, catch fish, and swallow them whole.

LAUNCHED INTO THE AIR

On the shore, Pteranodon would have moved awkwardly on all fours. Some scientists believe that Pteranodons would have launched themselves into the air from high rocks. Others believe they could have landed on, and then taken off from, the surface of the water, like modern-day gulls.

MICROLIGHT AIRCRAFT

Its wings were as wide as a microlight's, strengthened with gristle and supported with bone. With wings this size, Pteranodon would have flown without much flapping. In spite of its size, it could have moved quickly to snatch fish with ease.

THEN AND NOW

In the movie *Jurassic Park III*, Pteranodons are shown carrying people off in their claws. Could this really have happened? After examining fossilized Pteranodon bones and working out what muscle power they had, it's clear that they would not have been strong enough to do this. But they could have flown off carrying a large fish, just a like a modern eagle.

JUTTING-JAWED

PTEROSAURS

Pterosaurs' fearsome jaws came in all sorts of weird shapes. Some, like the Cearadactylus (see-AH-rah-DACK-till-us), had jaws similar to a crocodile's, while the jaws of Pterodaustro (TEH-roe-DAW-stroh) looked like those of a modern-day flamingo.

Other pterosaurs had spoonlike, upturned, or crested jaws. Pterosaurs adapted to make the best of their environments and to get the food they needed to survive. Their jaws were specially shaped to capture and eat fish, shellfish, insects, or carrion – so they had the perfect tools for crushing, sieving, and biting.

NO ESCAPE

At the end of Cearadactylus's crocodile-like jaws was a semicircle of interlocking needle-like teeth. Once caught, no fish could escape this deadly trap. The remaining teeth were small and less sharp. This suggests that it didn't bother with chewing and probably ate its catch whole.

TWEEZER-TIGHT

The jaw of the Dsungaripterus (SUNG-ah-RIP-ter-us) had an upturned tip, which could have been used to lever clinging shellfish from rocks. Farther back along the jaw there were bony, knob-like teeth. With the jaws shut tight, like tweezers or pliers, the knobs would have crushed the living prey from their shells.

A MEAN-LOOKING FLAMINGO?

The long, curved jaws of a Pterodaustro suggest that this pterosaur was a filter feeder, like a flamingo. Lowering its head to the water, it would scoop up surface water into its mouth. Anything living in the water would get stuck in the mass of 500 or so bristles in the lower jaw. Lots of little blunt teeth in the top jaw then brushed the food from between the bristles down its throat. As the food it probably ate, such as shrimps, was pinkish, its body may have been pink, just like a flamingo's.

PTERODAUSTRO VS FLAMINGO

	PTERODAUSTRO	FLAMINGO
BODY COVERING	Fur	Feathers
LENGTH	130 cm / 4 ft	106 cm / 42 in
WINGSPAN	3 m / 9 ft	1 m / 3 ft
WEIGHT	2-4.5 kg / 4.4-10 lb	2-4 kg / 4.4-8.8 lb

DIMORPHODON

TOOTH-BEAKED HUNTER

Dimorphodon (die-MORE-foe-don) was a fearsome fish- and insect-hunter. Its head was unusually big because of its deep jaws and mass of pointed teeth, which were ideal for impaling fish and carrying them off. It probably lived on cliffs or up trees, flying off to hunt for food and keeping away from predator dinosaurs.

BIG BITES
The deep beak allowed for large bites and big catches of fish. Such a big beak also made it easier to catch insects while flying. It may have been patterned for display, like a puffin's or a toucan's, perhaps showing off its presence during the breeding season.

FLAPPING FOR FISH
Dimorphodon wings were not as wide as some pterosaurs', so it may have needed to flap harder and faster to skim the seas.

CLINGING CLAWS
Dimorphodon had grasping claws on both its hands and its feet so that it could cling safely to tree trunks or the narrow ledges of sea cliffs.

LIGHT FOR FLIGHT

Dimorphodon's skull was large, but it contained empty spaces to make it light for flight. Although deep, its beak was narrow and streamlined so that it could cut through the air. If it rested on land, it probably crawled along on its two strong legs and wings. To take off, the wings were used for leverage – just as a pole-vaulter uses a pole to leap high.

MOUTH SPEARS

Dimorphodon's beak housed deadly weaponry. Its name means "two-form teeth" and this is because it possessed two types of teeth: the sides of its jaws were lined with up to 40 small, sharp teeth, and there were two larger, piercing teeth at the front.

DIMORPHODON VERSUS PUFFIN

	DIMORPHODON	PUFFIN
LENGTH	1 m / 3.3 ft	25 cm / 10 in
WINGSPAN	1.2-1.8 m / 4-6 ft	47- 63 cm / 19-25 in
WEIGHT	2267 g / 5 lb	500 g / 17.5 oz
FLIGHT SPEED	Unknown	88 kph / 55 mph
FEET	Clawed	Webbed

FURRY FIENDS

Rhamphorhynchoids were warm-blooded and probably furry, which makes them sound almost cute. But they certainly weren't friendly to the fish, insects, or other creatures they hunted.

As more types of rhamphorhynchoids appeared, their hunting and feeding tactics became more varied. Strange adaptations made them look like monsters, and scientists have looked for explanations for their bizarre body features.

KILLER TEETH

Jeholopterus (JAY-hole-OP-ter-us) was about the size of a house cat, with a 1-m (3-ft) wingspan. It had long, strong fangs in its top jaw, much larger than the rest of its teeth – like the fangs of a rattlesnake. Jeholopterus's claws were also sharper and larger than most other pterosaurs. Its jaws were built to open wide to snatch at insects in flight.

THEN AND NOW

Could Jeholopterus have been a bloodsucker, like a modern vampire bat? Some scientists have suggested that it may have used its long fangs to pierce the thick skin of dinosaurs and suck their blood. They say that it would have used its sharp claws to cling to the skin of the dinosaur while it attacked. However, there is little evidence to support this theory.

HAIRY HORROR

Even the name of this rhamphorhynchoid, Sordes (SORE-dess), is creepy. Sordes means 'filth' and is a reference to evil spirits in folk tales. It was named for its strange fur-like covering. Apart from a naked tail and wings, tiny hairs covered the whole of the creature's body. This led scientists to conclude that pterosaurs weren't cold-blooded killers at all – they were warm-blooded, like birds! As well as helping to keep them warm, a fur covering worked as a silencer, reducing the sound of its body in flight, so it could more easily take its prey by surprise.

QUETZALCOATLUS

GIANT VULTURE

Both terrifying and majestic, Quetzalcoatlus (KWET-zal-co-AT-lus) soared through the Late Cretaceous skies – the biggest flying creature known to have lived, and a giant compared with the biggest bird (the wandering albatross). For food, it may have plucked fish from the sea, torn at carrion, or probed in shallower lakes or shores for crustaceans and shellfish.

THE PLUMED SERPENT

Quetzalcoatlus is named after Quetzalcoatl, the mythical plumed serpent, worshipped by the ancient peoples of Mexico such as the Toltecs and Aztecs. Even though Quetzalcoatlus wasn't feathered, its slender jaws, long neck, head crest, and size would have given it an awesome appearance – even compared with the powerful dinosaurs of the time.

Quetzalcoatlus may even have preyed on small or baby dinosaurs. An injured dinosaur would have been a lucky find for such a colossal, hungry creature.

TRANSATLANTIC FLYER

Quetzalcoatlus was lightweight, with a skeleton of hollow bones, and it had no heavy teeth, yet it had massive wings. This meant it could travel greater distances, non-stop, than a passenger plane can today. Rising on warm air currents and gliding on breezes, it hardly needed to flap its wings. To find food, it could fly at speeds of 130 kph (80 mph) and for distances as great as 19,300 km (12,000 miles) – that's almost halfway around the world!

QUETZALCOATLUS VERSUS MICROLIGHT AIRCRAFT

	QUETZALCOATLUS	MICROLIGHT AIRCRAFT
WINGSPAN	11 m/36 ft	9 m / 30 ft
WEIGHT	100 kg /220 lb	300 kg / 661 lb
SPEED	130 kph /80 mph	250 kph / 156 mph

CRESTED COMPETITORS

Nyctosaurus (NICK-toe-SORE-us) had one of the longest head crests of all the pterosaurs. The bony, L-shaped growth was massive, with a length of 0.5 m (1 ft 7 in) – four times longer than its skull.

These mighty adornments may have been used to scare off other pterosaurs that were competing for the best feeding grounds. Just as stags use their antlers in fights during the mating season, the male Nyctosaurus may have used it to wage midair battles, swinging its crest like a sword as it wheeled through the air.

MISSING CLAWS
Mysteriously there were no claws on the second, third, and fourth fingers of Nyctosaurus's hands. Without these, it wouldn't have been able to cling to cliffs or trees, so probably spent most of its time patrolling the air.

SOARING AND WHEELING
The shape of Nyctosaurus's body and wings suggest that it was a top flier, able to turn sharply and capture air currents that would increase its speed as it soared.

FISH SKEWERS
The beak was long and sharply pointed to help it skewer fish as it dipped into the sea.

MINI FLYER

The small pterosaur, Tapejara (TOP-ay-HAR-ah), had a crest formed from two bones with a flap of skin stretched across. This was probably for display more than flight. It flew for short periods throughout the day and night, snapping up fish with its beak. The short, downturned beak was strong, and some scientists think its shape was adapted for eating fruit, not fish, while others think it may have been used to tear at the flesh of carcasses.

SKIN SAIL

Although there is no evidence from fossils, a skin attachment may have stretched across Nyctosaurus's crest like a sail. This could have been for display, or to help with aerodynamics. With a twist of the head a sail crest could have caught a breeze or air current, allowing for fast changes of direction in mid-air.

VITAL STATISTICS

NYCTOSAURUS

Meaning of name:
Night lizard

Family: Nyctosauridae

Period: Late Cretaceous

Size:
2.9 m / 9.5 ft wingspan

Weight: 5-10 kg / 11-22 lb

Diet: Fish

KEEN-EYED KILLERS

To catch fish, pterosaurs had to have sharp eyes, and brains that could respond quickly to what they saw, so they could home in on their kill. Anhanguera (ahn-han-GAIR-ah) had a large brain, so it was able to keep an eye on a swimming target, while co-ordinating its flight to successfully grab it.

SILLY LEGS
When Anhanguera sat down it would have looked rather odd. Its little legs would have spread out on either side of its body – they weren't built to be tucked neatly underneath like a bird's.

OLD DEVIL
In the Cretaceous period, pterosaurs evolved some strange-looking features. Anhanguera, which means "old devil", had crests at the far end of its top and bottom jaws. Its teeth were sharp and stuck out at the end, like a fishing net of bony spikes.

SENSITIVE WINGS
The wings sensed any air movements that might help or hinder its flight.

The fossilized skulls of pterosaurs give us information about the size and different parts of their brains. Large "optic lobes" show that their eyesight was good; smaller "olfactory lobes" suggest that pterosaurs did not have a strong sense of smell.

BIG

Ornithocheirus (or-nith-oh-CARE-us) had a wingspan of about 5 m (16 ft), making it the largest flying reptile of the Middle Cretaceous. It had crests on its beak, but unlike Anhanguera they had a semicircular shape and got thinner near the end. This may have helped it push its mouth through the water as it swam over the surface of the sea. Its teeth didn't stick out, so instead of a mouth like a fishing net, it had the weaponry to snap up larger fish.

BIRD-LIKE BITERS

The first bird-like creatures weren't like most of the birds we are familiar with today – they had vicious dino-like equipment, such as clawed wings and sharp, pointed teeth. Archaeopteryx (are-kee-OP-ter-ix) is the oldest known such creature, and lived with the dinosaurs in Jurassic times.

Archaeopteryx had feathers similar to those of today's birds, enabling it to fly. The feathers would also have helped insulate its body, keeping it warm and dry.

BRIGHT FEATHERS?

We know that some of Archaeopteryx's feathers were black, but like birds today they were probably brightly hued for communication, for example to attract a mate. We know that other prehistoric bird-like creatures, such as Sinosauropteryx (SIGH-no-sore-OP-ter-ix), had patterned feathers, and Archaeopteryx probably did as well.

LONG FINGERS

Its arms had developed into wings, but it still had finger claws, just as dinosaurs like Troodon did. It could probably fold its wings to its chest and overlap its claws.

BITING TEETH

Archaeopteryx was the size of a raven. But unlike modern birds, it had sharp, pointed teeth for biting and tearing at its prey.

BIG FEET

Big feet and toes enabled Archaeopteryx to grasp onto branches if necessary, but it could also walk along the ground on its strong legs to search for food.

BONY TAIL

Archaeopteryx's tail was bony rather than being made just of feathers. Its body was heavy compared to modern birds, so it wouldn't have been a good flier. For these primitive birds, flight may have been like extended leaping, flying for short bursts before gliding down to the ground again.

EARLY BEAKS

Confuciusornis (con-FEW-shus-OR-nis) didn't have teeth – it was one of the earliest birds to have a beak. Its beak may have been sharp enough to give a vicious a bite though, like a modern-day goose. It had the longest feathers, compared to its body, of all the known forerunners of birds. But the lack of a fan-shaped tail for flight probably meant that it wasn't an agile flier, especially at low speeds. Fossil remains show that its plumage had different hues, including red, brown, and black.

 ## FLYING MONSTER DETECTIVES

Archaeopteryx was an important discovery because it helped to show how birds developed from dinosaurs. It was a missing link in the evolutionary chain, possessing features of the theropod dinosaurs (a bony tail and sharp teeth) and features of today's birds (feathers and a forked bone between the neck and breast).

SEA MONSTERS

A giant sea turtle struggles to free itself from the deadly jaws of a ravenous Tylosaurus.

Some of the deadliest and weirdest-looking creatures that ever lived swam in prehistoric seas. There were fearsome "sea lizards" like Tylosaurus (TIE-low-SORE-us), huge turtles, terrifying sharks, massive-jawed ichthyosaurs (ICK-thee-oh-sores), and long-necked plesiosaurs (PLEH-see-oh-sores).

Top predators like Tylosaurus, a fast-swimming mosasaur (MOE-za-sore), were fearsome killers, easily devouring the largest of prey, like turtles and sharks. Tylosaurus may even have fed on dinosaur flesh, because Tylosaurus teeth marks have been found on the body of a hadrosaur (HA-dro-sore).

GIANTS OF THE OCEAN

The prehistoric ocean contained some giant versions of creatures familiar to us today. For example, Archelon (ARE-kell-on) was the biggest turtle ever known. About 4 m (13 ft) long and the weight of a family car, it had a leathery shell and snapped up prey like jellyfish and shelled creatures using its powerful, sharp-edged beak. Archelon may have lived for up to 100 years and perhaps even hibernated on the ocean floor.

SHELL SHOCK

By the Devonian period, prehistoric seas were teeming with weird-looking shelled creatures. The most well-known are the trilobites (TRY-low-bites) and ammonites (AM-mow-nites), because awesome fossils of their exoskeletons are often found.

Ammonites had spiral-shaped shells that could grow to huge sizes. Many of them, such as Oxynoticeras (OCKS-ee-NOT-i-SEER-us), were good swimmers, while others were slow-swimming bottom dwellers. They may have avoided predators by squirting ink, like today's octopuses and squid.

FLOATING AIDS

The ammonite's shell was strong enough to allow it to swim to great depths without being crushed by the pressure of the water. The inner chambers could be filled with gas to help the ammonite float upward when it wanted to rise.

BIG SOFTY

Just inside the entrance of the coiled shell lurked the soft body of this Hildoceras (HIL-doh-SEER-us) ammonite. It squirted jets of water from its body to whizz through the water, often moving around with others in large schools in search of food.

SQUASHING JAWS

Tentacles reached out to catch its food and then draw it up into its hidden mouth. It is believed that this monster survived on microscopic organisms called plankton.

TIGHT AS A BALL

The trilobites survived for more than 270 million years, scavenging, hunting, and filter-feeding on the ocean floor. There were many types of trilobite, now all extinct, but they are all related to the cockroaches and millipedes of today. They shed their protective exoskeleton several times as they got bigger, and a new one would grow in its place. Groups of up to 1,000 swarmed together so they could stay safe while waiting for their new shell to develop. Faced with danger, they curled up to keep their softer underbodies safe.

AMMONITES

VITAL STATISTICS

Meaning of name: Named after the Egyptian god Ammon

Family: Hildoceratidae

Period: Devonian to Cretaceous

Size: Up to 2 m (6.5 ft) diameter

Weight: 5–10 kg / 11–22 lb

Diet: Plankton

The spiral shell of the ammonite was divided into individual chambers. The creature lived in the largest, outermost of these chambers. When it became too big for a chamber, it grew another one and moved in there. Scientists estimate that it took about four weeks to grow a chamber, so they could grow around 13 per year. You can work out the age of an ammonite by counting the chambers in its shell.

CAMEROCERAS

TENTACLED TERROR

If you went for a swim in the Late Cambrian seas, you might be unlucky enough to encounter a spine-chilling Cameroceras (CAM-ur-oh-SEER-as). This massive squid-like monster may have been up to 9 m (30 ft) in length – the largest mollusk (soft-bodied invertebrate) ever known, and a top predator.

HUMONGOUS HORN

This creature's horn-shaped shell was made up of separated chambers, like an ammonite's (its name means "chambered horn"). As the animal grew, the shell grew to fit its increasing size. The animal lived in the top third of the shell, closest to the opening, so that it could reach out and grab its prey. Gas filled the shell chambers behind to help the creature move up and down in the seas.

Cameroceras probably fed on any prey that came within the reach of its terrifying tentacles, such as the jawless fish that inhabited the seas at that time.

A CANNIBAL?

Cameroceras is sometimes illustrated as a cannibal, eating its young. Scientists cannot be sure of their diet or how they hunted. Only their shells are found as fossils – all evidence of their soft bodies rotted away, leaving no lasting clues, such as stomach contents.

A TIGHT GRIP

Cameroceras had numerous long tentacles with sticky hooks, which it used to trap its prey.

TRACKING PREY

Like today's squid, Cameroceras may have tracked down its prey by picking up scents, or by using its pinhole eyes. Because it was so large, it may have stayed on the ocean floor, lying in wait to ambush passing creatures. Once spotted, the meal would be snatched, then pulled into its horny, beak-like mouth. There would have been little chance of escape.

THEN AND NOW

Estimates of the size of Cameroceras are based on a fossil of part of its shell. Scientists can guess at how it lived by studying related species that exist today, such as cuttlefish, octopus, and squid (such as this one).

FEARSOME SHARKS

Just as today, sharks were the greatest terrors of the seas in prehistory. But back then, sharks were even larger and deadlier. Weighing up to 100 tonnes (110 tons), Megalodon (MEG-ah-low-don) prowled the seas after the dinosaurs had died out and is the largest marine predator in the history of the planet.

Megalodon was longer than a school bus – that's three times longer than today's great white shark. Its teeth were over 15 cm (6 in) long and among the biggest choppers in the prehistoric world. Not only that, Megalodon had the most powerful bite of any creature that ever lived, with a bite force of 11–18 tonnes (12–20 tons) – enough to crush the skull of a whale.

SEA CREATURE DETECTIVES

Fossil teeth from prehistoric sharks were thought at first to be tongues because they were so big. A Megalodon tooth, such as this one, was similar to a great white's – triangular, sharp, and serrated. The serrations acted like the grooves in a saw, cutting through flesh as the shark shook its prey from side to side.

NO ESCAPE

Large fins allow for speedy turns, so Megalodon was an agile hunter. It may have chased whales to the surface when they needed to take a breath. The shark would attack from below and perhaps bite into the whale's underbelly before it could escape.

GIANT OF THE OCEANS

Megalodon's body is estimated to have been up to 20 m (65 ft) in length. From 25 to 1.6 million years ago, there was no ocean creature strong enough to compete with this monster shark.

KING-SIZE BITE

Megalodon's jaws were so vast a person would be able to stand up in its wide-open mouth. Its bite was so powerful that once it had a part of its prey in its mouth, like a fin, it would have been virtually impossible to escape. With an enormous hunger and a bite this size, huge whales would have been its target prey.

DINOSAUR BITES

Squalicorax (SKWA-lih-COR-ax) was a sharp-toothed shark that terrorized Cretaceous seas, feeding on smaller creatures like Enchodus (EN-coe-duss), a type of prehistoric fish. The foot bone of a hadrosaur was found with a Squalicorax tooth in it, suggesting that the shark was happy to turn scavenger and feed on a dead dinosaur that had been washed into the sea.

LONG-NECKED HUNTERS

Among the strangest looking monsters of the prehistoric seas were the elasmosaurs (el-LAZZ-moe-sores), a family of plesiosaurs with very long necks, which lived in Cretaceous waters. Their small heads were packed with sharp teeth that snatched up even the fastest-swimming prey. Their enormous stomachs are evidence of a massive appetite.

WEIGHTY BELLY

Elasmosaurs, like other plesiosaurs, ate stones. These are called gastroliths. Their weight may have helped their barrel-like bodies to stay stable.

BELLY STONES

We know that elasmosaurs ate stones because they have been found in fossils of these creatures. Gastroliths may have helped with digestion because as the elasmosaurs moved, the stones knocked against and mashed up the food they had eaten.

PADDLE POWER

Although elasmosaurs look ungainly, they were able to move their bodies up and down in a wave-like motion, similar to a swimming penguin, and flap their stiff paddles as if flying through the ocean. The front paddles were used for steering while the back ones produced the force to push their enormous bodies slowly through the water.

VITAL STATISTICS

ELASMOSAURUS

Meaning of name:
Ribbon lizard

Family: Elasmosauridae

Period: Late Cretaceous

Size: 12 m (40 ft) long

Weight:
2,000 kg / 2 tons

Diet: Fish

STICK YOUR NECK OUT

Albertonectes (al-BER-to-NEK-teez),
a type of elasmosaur, had a neck 7 m
(23 ft) in length – longer than any other
known plesiosaur. It had 76 neck vertebrae,
while mammals, including giraffes, only
have seven. Such a long neck enabled it to
grasp prey without having to swim far.

SNEAKY EATERS

The neck of Elasmosaurus, a type of elasmosaur, was so long
that, at first, scientists thought its neck fossils were part of a
tail. Elasmosaurus's long neck and small head were perfect
for sneaking up on schools of fish to eat. Elasmosaurus
reached out for fish, while keeping its bulky body well-
hidden in deeper, murky waters. The long, thin teeth that
stuck out from its mouth were like skewers.

LIOPLEURODON

JURASSIC TYRANT

Liopleurodon (LIE-oh-PLOOR-oh-don) is among the largest flesh-eating vertebrates ever to have lived. It was a short-necked plesiosaur – a voracious meat-eater and top hunter, which prowled the Jurassic seas for fish and other marine life, such as ichthyosaurs (ICK-thee-oh-sores) and squid.

The position of Liopleurodon's nostrils suggest that they were used for smelling, not breathing. The predator probably used its sense of smell to find its next meal, perhaps picking up on the presence of flesh or blood from long distances away. Its four powerful paddles would have given it a good chance of winning a chase, and its quick acceleration would have been ideal for ambushing prey.

TERRIFYING TEETH

With teeth the size of a T. rex's, Liopleurodon could take deadly bites, snapping at flesh or grabbing fish whole. Some of its teeth were 20 cm (8 inches) in length – the size of cucumbers – and stuck out at the front like a vicious animal trap. The huge head was a fifth of its body length and contained jaws powerful enough to hold onto a struggling Ichthyosaurus. Some experts believe it swam with its mouth open, catching any fish or squid that happened across its path.

LIOPLEURODON VERSUS TYRANNOSAURUS REX

	LIOPLEURODON	TYRANNOSAURUS REX
LENGTH	18 m / 59 ft	12 m / 39 ft
WEIGHT	25 tons	7.7 tons
JAW LENGTH	Over 3 m (9.8 ft)	1.2 m (4 ft)
PREY	Fish and other marine life	Meat
PERIOD	Mid-Late Jurassic	Late Cretaceous

POWER SWIMMERS

The pliosaurs (PLY-oh-sores) were cousins of the plesiosaurs with short necks, large heads, and massive, toothed jaws. They ranged from 4 to 15 m (13–49 ft) in length and preyed on fish, sharks, dinosaurs, and other marine reptiles.

TITAN OF THE SEA

Among the largest pliosaurs was Kronosaurus (crow-no-SORE-us). Named after the Greek titan Kronos, its big head, sturdy neck, and sharp teeth evoke the terrifying power of a mythical giant. Its huge, flat-topped skull made up a third of its body length and is bigger than the skull of any other known marine reptile. The pointed jaws hid rounded but deadly back teeth that could crush the shells of ammonites and turtles.

MUSCLE BOUND

There is evidence that Kronosaurus had strong muscles for swimming, so it was probably fast and agile in the water in spite of its bulky body.

DINO HUNTERS?

Pliosaurus (PLY-oh-SORE-us) was another giant pliosaur. Scientists estimate that its jaws would have been able to bite together with more force than those of a T. rex. The size of its teeth and the power of its jaws suggest that it may have had the strength to grab dinosaurs from the shore and devour them. Dinosaur bones have certainly been found in the stomachs of pliosauruses. However, these may have come from rotting dinosaur corpses, carried by the tide or a river into the ocean.

SEA MONSTER DETECTIVES

Sometimes only a few parts of a sea monster are discovered. Working out which part belongs where can be a bit like doing a jigsaw puzzle. Another challenge is classifying these creatures. This is a Trinacromerum (TRY-nack-roe-MARE-um), a type of plesiosaur – but it was originally mistaken for another, similar-looking species of plesiosaur called a Dolichorhynchops (DOE-lih-co-RIN-cops).

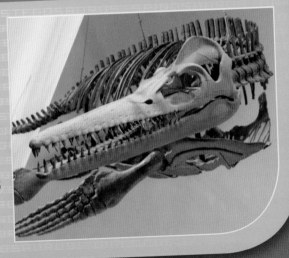

ICHTHYOSAURS

FISH-LIZARDS

The ichthyosaurs (ICK-thee-oh-sores), or "fish-lizards", looked a little like dolphins, but they were more like killer sharks. These reptilian hunters of Jurassic times boasted a fearsome set of jaws.

Ichthyosaurs like Excalibosaurus (ex-CAL-ih-bo-SORE-us) and Ichthyosaurus (ICK-thee-oh-SORE-us) were awesome swimmers and well-adapted to hunt for prey, or scavenge if necessary.

SHARK-LIKE HUNTERS

The 2 m (6.6 ft) long Ichthyosaurus had a dolphin-shaped body but its tail looked more like a shark's. It also lived like a shark, hunting in deep, open waters. The long, tooth-filled jaws snapped up shellfish, fish, and squid.

BEADY EYES

Ichthyosaurus's eyes were extra large to help pick up what light they could in the murky ocean depths.

HUNTING SPEED

Two sets of flippers and a dorsal fin stabilized the Ichthyosaurus as it swam. It propelled itself through the water with flicks of its tail, moving quickly thanks to its body's streamlined shape.

SWORD-LIP

Some ichthyosaurs, like Excalibosaurus, had a longer, sword-like upper jaw and looked a bit like a swordfish. Excalibosaurus is named after Excalibur, King Arthur's mythical sword. Its "sword" might have been used as a probe to dig for food on the ocean floor. Or it may have been used as a weapon in battles or to capture its prey. The part of the top jaw that extended beyond the lower jaw was lined with rows of outward-facing teeth, which would have been deadly if stabbed into the flesh of its prey or an enemy reptile.

EXCALIBOSAURUS VERSUS SWORDFISH

	EXCALIBOSAURUS	SWORDFISH
LENGTH	7 m / 23 ft	3 m / 9.8 ft
WEIGHT	907 kg / 2,000 lb	650 kg / 1,430 lb
TEETH	On upper and lower jaw	No teeth in adults
PREY	Fish, other marine life and reptiles	Fish, squid, octopus
PERIOD	Late Jurassic	Now

FISH FANGS

Sharks were not the only deadly prehistoric fish. Some, like Dunkleosteus (DUNK-lee-owe-STEE-us), were powerful enough to attack and kill a shark. Other predatory fish, such as Enchodus (EN-coe-duss), make today's piranhas look positively friendly.

WELL PROTECTED

Dunkleosteus had tough, protective plating to shield its enormous 10-m (33-ft) long, 3-tonne (3. 3 ton) body against other hunters in the Devonian seas. Bite marks on these fish suggest that they sometimes turned to cannibalism when other food was hard to find.

MEAT SLICERS

Instead of teeth, Dunkleosteus had slicing, bony plates. It bit hard with one part of its jaw, capturing even powerful, struggling prey.

JAWS!

Dunkleosteus had a greater biting force than a great white shark. Its bone-crushing jaws had a force of 500 kg (1100 lbs) – more than twice as powerful as a hyena's.

SHARP-TOOTHED KILLERS

Enchodus, which lived in the Late Cretaceous, could almost be mistaken for a modern salmon or herring – except for its mouthful of huge, sharp teeth. At the front of its mouth were two piercing fangs that could grow up to 6 cm (2.4 in) in length. These fangs, together with its large eyes, made it a formidable hunter. Like many types of fish, it might have lived and hunted in schools. A school of these fang-mouthed monsters could have overcome marine creatures far bigger than themselves.

 **SEA MONSTER** DETECTIVES

Three-dimensional computer models of extinct monsters like Dunkleosteus are created to discover more about how they moved and hunted. A computer model of Dunkleosteus revealed that it could open its jaws in just a fiftieth of a second – fast enough to have created a suction force capable of pulling passing prey into its mouth.

GIANT CROCS

Swamps, lakes, rivers, and estuaries were dangerous places for small land animals to wander. Even huge dinosaurs were at risk of a surprise attack from one of the giant crocodiles that lurked there. Bite marks on dinosaurs, including the massive carnivore Albertosaurus, reveal attacks from Deinosuchus (DIE-no-SOO-kuss), one of the biggest crocodiles to exist.

Prehistoric crocodiles were probably even more terrifying than modern-day crocs. Gigantic creatures like the "supercroc" Sarcosuchus (sar-co-SOOK-us) and Deinosuchus (which means "terrible crocodile") hid in shallow waters, waiting to ambush their prey.

HORRIFIC!

Deinosuchus had huge jaws with about 44 sharp teeth, and it had a horrific bite, more powerful than some of the biggest dinosaurs. With a 10-m (33-ft) long body, and a skull longer than an adult human is tall, this monster must have had quite an appetite, so a large dinosaur was probably a tempting meal. It lived in river mouths, where it also snapped up turtles and fish.

SUPERCROC

The length of a bus and the weight of a small whale, Sarcosuchus, nicknamed "supercroc", was the biggest crocodile-like creature ever known, and twice the size of any crocodile living today. Its teeth were rounded, and built for grabbing at prey and crushing, not for taking bites. It probably lay half-submerged in shallow rivers, dining on large fish and any other prey that wandered by. It may also have crawled onto land to tuck into the remains of carrion, left over from a dinosaur kill. Sarcosuchus had a peculiar bulbous tip at the end of its snout, called a bulla. Scientists don't know what this was for, but it may have helped it make sounds, or enhanced its sense of smell.

VITAL STATISTICS

SARCOSUCHUS

Meaning of name:
Flesh crocodile

Family: Pholidosauridae

Period: Early Cretaceous

Size: 12 m (40 ft) long

Weight: 9,000-13,600 kg / 10-15 tons

Diet: Fish and carrion

GLOSSARY

breeding season Months in the year when creatures gather to mate in order to have offspring.

browsing (A herbivore) feeding on shoots, leaves, and other plant matter.

camouflage Markings or patterns that help something to blend into its setting so that it cannot be easily seen.

Carboniferous A prehistoric period when there were many swamps and forests. Fossil fuels later formed from the trees and plants that died.

carcass The body of a dead creature.

carrion Flesh from a creature that has died, and a source of food for some birds and animals.

ceratopsians A group of large, four-legged dinosaurs, most of which had horns and frills.

clam A large shellfish with two main parts to its shell, similar to an oyster.

crest A body part that sticks up from an animal's head and may be ornamental.

Cretaceous A prehistoric period during which mammals and giant dinosaurs lived, and which ended with the mass extinction of the dinosaurs 65 million years ago.

Devonian A prehistoric period, also known as the Age of Fishes, when the oceans were warm and filled with many types of evolving fish.

dorsal fin An upright flipper rising up from the back of a fish and used for steering and stability.

evolve To change gradually over time.

extinct Not existing anymore.

filtering Extracting food, such as tiny fish from water, by passing it through sieve-like parts of the mouth.

flamingo A pink or reddish wading bird with long legs, a long neck, and a duck-like bill.

flippers Limbs used by creatures in the water for swimming.

food chain A group of organisms arranged in order of rank, with each dependent on the next as a source of food. For example, a fox eats a mouse, the mouse eats an insect, and the insect eats a plant.

fossil The remains of a prehistoric organism preserved in rock.

fossilized Made into a fossil.

frill A bony area around the neck of a dinosaur.

gills The parts of a fish's body that are used for breathing.

grazing Feeding on low-growing plants.

hadrosaurs Plant-eating family of dinosaurs, also known as duck-billed dinosaurs because of their beak-like mouths.

herbivore A plant-eater.

hibernating Spending the winter in a dormant (slowed-down or inactive) state.

ichthyosaurs A group of large, sea-living reptiles that looked similar to dolphins.

insulation A way of keeping heat in and cold out.

invertebrate A creature without a backbone, such as a worm, a squid, or an insect.

Jurassic A prehistoric period in which many large dinosaurs lived. It is also called the Age of Reptiles.

mosasaur A giant, meat-eating, and sea-living family of reptiles that used four paddle-like limbs to swim.

omnivorous A diet of both plants and meat.

pachycephalosaurids A family of two-legged dinosaurs that had very thick, sometimes domed, skulls.

palaeontologist A scientist who studies fossil animals and plants.

plates Bony sections on the surface of a dinosaur that gave it protection. Some plates stood up from the spine, as on a Stegosaurus.

plesiosaurs A group of reptiles that evolved to live in the sea and used paddle-like limbs to swim.

predator An animal that hunts other animals to kill and eat.

prey An animal that is hunted by other animals for food.

pterosaurs A group of flying reptiles that were closely related to the dinosaurs.

reptiles Cold-blooded animals that usually lay eggs and have scales.

sauropods A group of giant, four-legged plant-eating dinosaurs with small heads, long necks and tails.

serrated Having a jagged, saw-like edge.

spinosaurids A family of two-legged, meat-eating dinosaurs that lived in the Cretaceous period.

streamlined Something that is smoothly shaped, enabling it to move easily through, for example, woods, water, or air.

therapods A group of two-legged, mainly meat-eating dinosaurs, such as Tyrannosaurus rex and Giganotosaurus.

titanosaur A type of enormous sauropod.

Triassic A prehistoric period during which the first dinosaurs and mammals evolved.

vertebrate A creature with a backbone, such as a bird, mammal, or reptile.

wingspan The measurement across the wings of an animal, such as a bird or a pterosaur, when the wings are outstretched.

INDEX